EASTWARDS,

OR

REALITIES OF INDIAN LIFE

BY

C. P. A. OMAN,

LATE OF TIRHOOT, BENGAL.

London:

SIMPKIN, MARSHALL & Co.,
Paternoster Row.

PRINTED BY

F. C. HARRISON,

24, *Queen's Terrace, St. John's Wood.*

MDCCCLXIV.

CONTENTS.

CONTENTS.

CHAPTER VIII.

CHAPTER IX.

CHAPTER X.

CHAPTER XI.

CHAPTER XII.

CHAPTER XIII.

CHAPTER XIV.

EASTWARDS,

OR

REALITIES OF INDIAN LIFE.

CHAPTER I.

INTRODUCTORY.

ON a mild, sunshiny morning, in the month of May, might be seen, sauntering up the promenade of one of our fashionable spas, two pale little children, who ever and anon turned to the black ayah with them, and prattled some outlandish words, much to the amusement of the other nursemaids who were on duty at the same place. The poor ayah looked a miserable object in her thin semi-English dress, and, no doubt, was longing to return to her dearly-beloved land of curry and rice, hookahs and pawn.

The two children are the hero and heroine of our story. The boy is about six, and well grown, but has not the clear complexion or plump limbs of an English-born child. There is no doubt, however, of his pure Anglo-Saxon origin, which is

1

written clearly on his high forehead, in his light-gray green eye, and curly brown hair.

The girl is a tiny wee thing of four years, and seems weak in her ankles. A year or two more, and her career would have been finished in that cruel India. She has sweet little features, bright blue eyes, and auburn hair; a gentle, timid thing now, and likely to be so hereafter, if voice, and feature, and gesture are any indications of her future.

They are joined presently by two grave, elderly ladies, dressed alike in dark colours, who stooped to kiss the little ones, and then speak a word of encouragement to grumbling old Mooneah, for whom they feel great pity and are detaining till they can get her a ship, and another nurse can supplant her in the affections of the children.

"Well, Mooneah, how are the babas (children) to-day? (They know a word or two of Hindostanee, you see.) Their colour seems much better; eh, ayah? Do you feel cold You really ought to give up wearing those thin slippers. How do you like the shawl we gave you? Is it warm enough?"

"Ah, Mem Saheb," drawled out the black woman, "shawl bery good, but I not like dis contree; no bazar, no curry, no smoke hookah. When ship be ready to take Mooneah back?"

"Very soon, ayah; you shall go, if possible, in the vessel which brought you here. She will be ready to sail nex month."

"Now, Hampton ; now, Laura," said they, addressing the children, "let us see how fast you can run to that big chesnut tree."

The little pair do their best, while their aunts watch, with newly-awakened interest, their anything but effective display of activity. "They will do better by and bye, won't they, Catherine ?" said Aunt Jane. " Poor things ! how weak they are."

Our little friends are the children of Major Templemore, an officer in the Bengal army. He had seen his other little ones dwindle and die from the effects of climate, and was determined, if possible, to save the two last by sending them to England early. They were entrusted to the care of his maiden sisters, who were prepared to show them all the kindness that affection for their brother, and pity for the two delicate little creatures, could produce in their susceptible hearts. The children's mother died a few months before they left India, and they have little recollection of her. Sometimes, in after years, Laura fancied she could recall her sweet wan face as she watched their gambols of an evening on that, to them, delicious play-ground, the terrace of their house at Delhi. But it may have been only fancy, for the portrait left to aid her memory was taken years before, and represented a pretty rosy English girl.

Often did the sensitive little Indian child wish that she could have lavished on her mother that love, which she knew she could have shown, had Providence spared her a few years

longer. This thought, however, she felt was almost ungrate-
ful to her aunts, for no mother could have been more loving
or attentive to their little charges than they were. Hampton
was not of such an imaginative temperament as his sister, and
though her senior, seemed sooner to forget his parents, and all
the little incidents of his babyhood. He had, indeed, an indistinct idea of his father being a soldier, ever so high, say
seven feet, commanding an army of one hundred thousand
black sepoys. Then he jumbled up snakes, cockroaches, and
green lizards, with the tame leopards kept by the King of
Delhi for hunting antelopes in the adjacent plains, which
his father had once taken him to see. And, by the
bye, he did remember his mother's old ayah, Sookeah, and
that ugly old sirdar-bearer who played with him from morning to night, and was called by the euphonious name of
Ramoo.

Years rolled by, and still Major Templemore remained in
India. Enticed by that terrible ignis fatuus, the emoluments
of a staff appointment, he lingered on and on till one day,
when Laura was about twelve years old, a letter was handed
to the elder Miss Templemore at breakfast time, after opening
which she became deadly pale, and gave a glance at her sister,
who rose and accompanied her from the room. A vague
terror seized the two children; a sense of some undefined evil
filled their minds, the remembrance of which often recurred
to them in after years, and was the more deeply imprinted on
their memories from the day being a bright summer's one, on

which they had been invited to join a joyous party in a pic-
nic to Dowdeswell wood.

Their aunts did not come back, so Laura followed them,
and softly crept into the drawing-room, which was nearly
dark from the shutters being closed. She found them silently
weeping, and was not rebuked for coming into the room un-
bidden. They took her fondly between them, and, bending
over her, kissed her gently, while one of them whispered,
"You are now an orphan, indeed, Laura. God has taken
your father away." Those who have not been separated from
their parents in childhood cannot feel as the sensitive little
Laura did. Were her bright dreams fled, lost, gone for ever?
Was she never to cling round papa's neck, as she had often
pictured herself doing? never to talk to him about long lost
mamma, and what they used to do in that to her fairy land,
far off India? Were they never to walk through green lane or
shady wood together, she showing him the way and gathering
sweet-scented wild flowers? Was he never to call her his
darling and his blossom, and make her wild with joy by his
tenderly shown love? These thoughts were more than she
could bear, and she sank unconscious into her aunts' arms. In
a day or two, when she was more composed, they read her the
letter, which was a very kind one. It said that Major Templemore had died from a low fever acting on an enfeebled constitution, and that he had left his property equally divided in
trust for his children, in the hands of the writer, his brother
George, who was a civilian in Bengal. Enclosed were a few

lines from his wife, of formal condolence, and an invitation
which amounted to a command, for Laura to join her when she
was seventeen. Hampton was to have a nomination to Addiscombe when he was old enough, through the influence of a
cousin of his father's, who was a director, and a man of influence in London.

Time did not thoroughly efface her sore trial from Laura's
mind, but the lines written on the tablets of her memory
gradually grew fainter. Were this not so we should be
crushed by our very first grief, and the world's great chorus,
in which the song is made providentially to drown the sigh,
would be one mournful dirge. Hampton showed some of his
sister's feelings, but he was more stolid than she was, and
although not wanting in kindness of heart, he could not
realise the amount of grief which she felt, and was consoled
much sooner. He joined the Cheltenham College about this
time, and the novelty and excitement of his position soon
weaned his thoughts from the past to be centred on the future—
the hopeful glorious future. Laura was not sent to any school,
and was brought up in a quiet unsophisticated way by her
aunts, who were very children in the world's stratagems, and
dreaded to think that their darling should become a mere
milliner's dummy. She had overcome all the little delicacies
of constitution engendered by her being born in India, and at
sixteen was as graceful a specimen of womanhood as ever
charmed the eye of devoted parent, or enchained the fancy of
chivalrous youth. Her voice was sweet as distant music, her

every movement told of bounding health and strength and youthful symmetry ; she had not, as yet, been blown upon by the world's corrupting breath, and her clear, unshrinking, yet modest glance, told of the innocence of her mind. Hampton's physical energy, we are obliged to confess, was decidedly superior to his mental, and by the time he was eighteen he was a fine strapping fellow. Who does not, of his quondam schoolfellows, remember the awful kick he gave the football in that grand match, when he flattened bully William's nose, disfiguring that young gentleman for nearly a fortnight. Who has forgotten his tremendous scores at cricket, or that terrific fight he had with the grammar-school boy, who was half a head higher than himself, and weighed fully one stone more ?

In due course Hampton went to Addiscombe, finished his studies there, and was appointed an infantry cadet on the Bengal establishment. It was arranged that he should go out overland with his sister, whose departure was now at hand. He returned to Cheltenham for a month or two, and was delighted to renew his old acquaintances; not a little proud was he also to show off before his former schoolfellows, who on their part felt highly honoured by his notice. Laura found that the kind of halo which surrounded her, as one fated to go to India, was not such a charming fact, when she had to fulfil her destiny in reality. She looked upon her aunts with the fondest affection, and the beauties of the spot she had spent her childhood in, had twined themselves imperceptibly round her heart. But go she must. Often did her sorrowing aunts

deplore their want of means to adopt and maintain her in her
proper sphere in England, but such was not to be her lot, and
they yielded up the solace of their old age with bitter, hopeless regrets. The outfit buying was a sorrowful affair, and
Laura's young friends must have thought her most un-
natural for not taking more interest in the pretty things
selected.

At last all was ready. Brother and sister knew the day when
they were to join in London a Madras civilian and his wife ;
the latter of whom was to act as Laura's special protectress,
as far as Madras, whence a four days' trip would take her to
Calcutta, where her uncle George awaited her arrival. There
is not much more to tell of our heroine before leaving Cheltenham. She had lived such a quiet secluded life with her aunts
that she had enjoyed little opportunity of creating any
romances, such as she used to be entertained with by her fair
companions. But do not fancy, young ladies, that she had not
pictured the ideal prince, who was one day to come and woo
her ; and that, failing that sweet and illustrious individual,
she had not thought that she might reasonably be content
with somebody like handsome Conrad Daymer, who sat in
church near her, and who used to steal a glance at her now
and then during service, making her (I am sorry to say)
think more of the effect of her Sunday bonnet than the
sermon. There is little doubt that the meeting at the church
door was also contrived, although she only suspected it then.
The way, too, in which he stopped that great plunging horse

of General Feebul's, when it was about to run over aunt Jane and herself, was decidedly heroic, and of course she admired him greatly for his prowess. This incident led to a closer intimacy, and the acquaintanceship gradually ripened into friendship ; but she was very young, and love—with all its absorbing force—had as yet only gently touched her heart. What effect time and separation had upon her feelings will be seen in the progress of our story.

It is needless to describe the painful parting of our youthful travellers from their dearly loved aunts. The latter would not see them, the morning they went to the railway ; and all concerned tried to console themselves with the idea, that they should write *so often*, India was so close now, and a dozen other sophistries of the like character. Hampton doubled himself up in a corner of the railway carriage, and wished those fellows from the college had not come to see him off, for he knew he was almost crying, and it would never do for them to report such a thing of the game Templemore. Our heroine hid her tears beneath a thick veil, and could not give any very distinct reply to a soft voice, which, just as they were starting, said, " Good bye, Laura, God bless you ! I shall soon bring you some late news from Cheltenham, as in another month or two I shall probably be on the road to India." These were Conrad Daymer's last words, and he seemed as miserable as she was. Sometimes in deep thought, sometimes shedding bitter tears, Laura was landed at her chaperon's residence in London, by her brother, who, after a hasty introduction to

Mr. and Mrs. Chàntney, and a hurried farewell to his sister,
went off to an hotel in the neighbourhood.   Here for a while
their routes became different, as Hampton was to go in a
steamer with the heavy luggage from Southampton, while she
journeyed across France a few days later, with her new friends,
meeting again at Alexandria. Mrs. Chantney was quite an old
Indian in her appearance and manners, although she was not
at all an old woman. She had that worn, haggard look,
which Englishwomen acquire after a long residence in the
tropics, and was dressed fashionably and yet carelessly. She
was much less stiff, our heroine thought, than untravelled
Englishwomen generally are, and altogether had a slightly
foreign air, which rather pleased than otherwise. She seemed
satisfied with her young companion's appearance, and very
soon commenced a series of lectures concerning her conduct on
board ship, &c. " You know, my dear," she said, " without
any flattery, you are very nice looking, and there are always
a number of good for nothing young officers on board these
steamers, who will try to persuade you that they are ready to
jump overboard for your sake, while the truth is they are
probably engaged to some confiding girl in England, or have
sworn the same vapid oaths to every one they have danced
with ; and in fact have been so spoiled by the way the young
women go on now-a-days, that they are insufferable. India
is the place to put a stop to that kind of thing. Fifty men
and twenty women only in a ball-room, soon brings Mr.
Jackanapes to his senses, and young ladies learn to value

themselves a little more, and can pick and choose exactly in the way the men do here. Oh! you will find it quite delicious after the experience you have had at home."

Laura pretended to be very knowing indeed, but in truth she hardly knew what Mrs. Chantney was talking about, for she had not been out to many balls or parties, and her mind was as unsophisticated as the good example and training of her aunts could make it. She did not see much of Mr. Chantney, who seemed to be a harmless individual, with a great aptitude for smoking, and who had a fixed idea that he was thrown away in India, whereas, if he had been allowed to work his way in England, he would have been at the head of his profession; the probability being that, having neither application nor talent, he would never have earned more than a hundred or two a year, as a clerk. He did, however, very well for the land of ryot warree settlements, and other benighted isms.*

Mrs. Chantney had a decided objection to the sea route from Southampton *via* the Bay of Biscay, and intended to go slowly through France. So Laura had the pleasure of admiring its gay capital, buying a beautiful silk or two at Lyons, and exploring the environs of Marseilles for a couple of days. The steamer which took them to Alexandria was unusually crowded, December being a favorite month for making the dreaded journey down the Red Sea, and our heroine began to realise some of the incidents which Mrs.

* Madras is called the benighted presidency by Bengalese.

Chantney had told her were likely to happen. There, true
enough, were the newly-married couples, who had commenced
their honeymoon in France, and who made themselves so
painfully ridiculous by their billing and cooing. Then there
there was a grumpy old general, three or four civilians and
their wives, a tough-looking old Scotch doctor, several
married ladies *en route* to join their husbands, two or three
spinsters, a dozen officers of all ages and sizes, some Dutchmen
and their families for Batavia, and last, though not least, a
French commandant of troops serving in China, with Monsieur le Baron attached to the diplomatic corps there, and a
romantic little French doctor for Pondicherry. Sixty
passengers in all, but what were these to the crowd they will
join at Alexandria? not less than a hundred more, they were
told, made up from every nation in Europe. Can a more
amusing scene than the deck of an overland route steamer,
under these circumstances, be imagined? splendid weather, a
well supplied table, and a magnificent vessel careering along
at the rate of twelve or thirteen knots an hour, are enough to
put everyone in the highest spirits; and it is no wonder that
some wild pranks are played now and then in Egypt, by the
younger passengers, who are half mad with excitement and
the novelty of their position. A beautiful day saw them
cutting through the sparkling waves of the Mediterranean,
off the South of France. Fine weather accompanied them
the whole way, and bright moonlight shone on Malta's walls
as they entered its romantic harbour. Here a few hours'

delay enabled Laura to see the usual lions, buy some light lace articles for her aunts, write them a hasty line or two, and then they were off again for Alexandria.

Having dismissed our heroine from Malta, we must allow Hampton Templemore to describe *his* fortunes after leaving Southampton. This he did in a letter to an old schoolfellow and friend, John Sterndell, who had passed through the Cheltenham College, and was preparing for Cambridge previous to entering himself at the Bar.

"OFF SOUTHAMPTON, *on board the P. and O. Steamer,*
December 4th, 185—.

" MY DEAR JACK,—Here I am in the greatest bustle and confusion I ever experienced. There are over one hundred passengers of all sorts, sexes, and sizes. They have shoved me into a hole with three other cadets, two of whom were my detestation at Addiscombe. One of them, Binkey, is a horrid snob, couldn't play at cricket or anything ; the other is a sneak ; I am convinced he once peached on my being at Croydon, when I ought not. If I can only manage to let in a heavy sea on them some day or other, through the port, I shall be happy. The third is in the Engineers, very studious, and can't smoke a bit. We have two small basins to wash in, and the allowance of water may be guessed by the diminutive size of the jugs. How they manage to feed and attend on us all I don't know. There are a host of cooks, and twenty

stewards, who balance plates and knives at dinner like
Chinese jugglers—still it must be hard work. One of the
mates tells me I ought to see them on the Indian side with
the thermometer at 100°. He says they are walking shower-
baths, and only live three years, not pleasant is it ? There is
great fun on board. I intend to keep this open till we reach
Malta, and write a little each day.

"December 5th.—Nearly had a fight with Binkey, who
sleeps opposite me, about which of us should wash first.
Told him to behave like an officer and a gentleman, and that
he could find me whenever he wanted me. The row ended,
I am sorry to say, in my threatening to throw him out of the
port, which is impossible. Made friends to-day with a fellow
in the Queen's, he has been to India before, and is a
regular brick; he has some of the primest baccy I ever
smoked. He says cadets are called griffs, and warns me not
to make a fool of myself. I shall do my best. There is such
a pretty girl on board with her mother; I must try and get
some one to introduce me.

"6th.—There are rats in the cabin. They have stolen all
our socks. By Jove! is it the steward ? If it is, and we
catch him, look out, that's all. Introduced to Miss Danvers
(the pretty girl) and her mother to-day; strange to say,
Mrs. Danvers was at school with aunt Jane. We are awfully
thick now. I wonder if an ensign could manage to keep a wife.

"7th.—Rough sea to-day. All in our cabin very bad.
Steward swears he won't bring in the mop any more. I don't

sleep under the port. Such a sea came in this morning, right over my two enemies, who do—

"8th.—A little better to-day. Fanny Danvers on deck again, looking pale but lovely. Could have annihilated an old major with a beard like a chimpanzee, who would speak to her. She said he was so annoying.

"9th.—Expect to get into Gibraltar to-morrow early. The coast of Spain very grand at the Straits, must get up to see it. Have some foreigners and their wives on board; they eat like ogres. One of the wives devours red hot chutney in a way that would astonish a salamander. Some of the young men drink beer at dinner and luncheon in a shameful manner; it looks as if they never saw it at home.

"10th.—Got up at six; paddled about the wet decks. The cliffs at the entrance of the Straits are magnificent, and crowned by old monasteries and other striking buildings. Got into Gibraltar at about nine o'clock. Went on shore, with my chum the Engineer. Looked over the lower fortifications; didn't see much in them. My companion said they were very strong, and he ought to know. Must be a terrible sore to the proud Don to have so many John Bulls quartered near him. Blows very hard, always blows at Gibraltar; very nearly swamped getting on board.

"11th.—Left Gibraltar yesterday evening. Expect to get to Malta by the 13th. The weather is beautiful, like our English spring. Mrs. Danvers asked me to-day how old I was, and whether I was in the civil service; said no, and that I preferred honour to pay. She said oh! and then remarked, it was a pity infantry officers were so ill paid, as they could not expect to marry and be respectable for a number of years. Felt my face get rather red, and thought her an old fool.

"12th.—Forgot to tell you that we have a band on board, formed from among the stewards. They play very fairly, indeed. The first violin is quite a genius,—paints little sketches on the tops of the music programmes, and is a ventriloquist. One of the civilians on board has got hold of Fanny Danvers, and she seems to enjoy his attentions. I never noticed she had such large feet before.

"13th.—In this morning to Malta. Not a green thing to relieve the snuffy-brown look of the rock, except of course the town itself, which is white, and is a huddled up mass of terraces, steeples, and fortifications. The harbours are like old quarries, filled with water, deep, awfully deep. The streets leading from them up to the town, are nothing but staircases under a false name. The principal features of life are lace and oranges, with a dash of coral, bad jewellery, and Canary birds. The horses (barbs from Africa) are very pretty. The natives are regular Moors. Went to see the old Knight Templars' Church of St. John's. You push aside a curtain, and are in the centre of the place in a moment. Women with black silk mantillas thrown over their heads, and brigand-looking peasants in velvet and buttons are dotted about the floor, kneeling. A group of priests are performing some service at the altar. Horribly out of keeping with the above are two or three parties from the steamer, with that fiery red face which Englishmen have when they go sight-seeing, and a look generally as if they were struggling not to laugh—it is such bad taste! The proportions of the building, the Mosaic pavement and ornaments are splendid. An old picture over one of the arches, monk or saint I don't know which, particularly struck me. Saw the last Grand Master, Lisle Adam's tomb, and the solid silver altar rails, which were whitewashed over and saved, when the French had possession. Then to the church of the Capuchins to see the dried mummies of departed Fathers, stuck up in niches in the wall, a disgusting and purposeless display, for if any thoughts are engendered in the mind, they are those of contempt for our species as exemplified in those laughable old skeletons. I shall write you again from Ceylon; say everything that is kind to my old schoolfellows and friends, and with every good wish in this life for you and yours,

"I am, old boy, yours affectionately,

"HAMPTON TEMPLEMORE.

"P.S.—I forgot to say that we met a number of water-spouts. One of them was so close that our course had to be altered. We could see the water gyrating up the inverted cone, as distinctly as possible, and hear the roar as the waves lashed each other into fury at its point of junction with the sea. It was going at a tremendous pace, and would swamp a fleet if it caught it."

CHAPTER II.

EGYPT—THE RED SEA.

ALL the way from Marseilles, the little French doctor, whom we introduced to our readers in our last, had been most attentive to Mrs. Chantney and her charge; and as he was scrupulously respectful and polite, the former saw no harm in accepting his "petits soins." In fact she was highly amused at the account Laura used to give in the cabin of the admiration he expressed for her.

"You are une dame distingué; of such a noble air, and you talk such beautiful French."

Then, in return, Mrs. Chantney told Laura that he was dying of love for *her*.

"You are so gentle, so beautiful a blonde; *you* are the real attraction," she said laughingly, "and I should not wonder if he throws himself at your feet some evening, in a dark corner, and vows to win you or die. He has already brought out a volume of thrilling French poems, some of which he has read to me, till the tears rolled down his great black beard, and he is going to try their effect on you in the Red Sea. Have you not also heard a deep voice singing imploring love songs somewhere near the gangway after dark? That's the doctor, my dear, and all that pathos is directed at you, so take care of your heart, I warn you."

Two others of her fellow passengers had been marked by Laura from the first, and she had taken rather a dislike to them; one was a Captain Desmond, and the other a bold, fast-looking, *youngish*, young lady, whose name she discovered to be Constance Browning.

Desmond was one of your military admirable Crichtons, who seem to be able to do everything. He was decidedly good-looking, could play on two or three instruments, draw and dance well. One of those men who are always going to sell out, or about to exchange; bolting from their creditors, or suddenly very flush of cash; now in the Guards, and again in a West India regiment; going to be married, till the brother comes home and fights a duel with him; or, if married, divorced from his wife, who is notorious in London. He seemed to think that Laura must at once be fascinated by his attractions; but somehow or other she did not like the sinister blasé look in his eyes, and treated him with perfect indifference.

Not so Miss Browning.

Perhaps she had never seen a man of his calibre before, or perhaps only with the craving for excitement of a confirmed man-hunter, she did all she could to secure his attention to herself. He, however, seemed more struck with our heroine's innocent fresh look and manner, than with Miss Browning's bolder style, and took much trouble in cross-examining Mrs.

Chantney as to her destination and antecedents. That lady, who had a strong inclination for match-making, gave him the most glowing account of everything she knew, and hinted that Miss Templemore was quite an heiress.

Laura could not help noticing Captain Desmond's manner to her; and as she mused on the incidents of the last few days, thought it so strange that she, yesterday but a school-girl, should to-day be called on to join the battle of life, and that she should so naturally fall into the ranks and do her devoir with the best. The fact is that a trip, such as the one to India, changes the thoughtless girl into the thinking woman, in a day, so to speak. And lucky is she who has good advice and kind protection to enable her to avoid being led away by the false excitement of the situation. A girl who perhaps has never had any particular attention paid to her, suddenly finds herself a perfect heroine; and many a heart-ache is the result, when the break-up of the party takes place, and she discovers herself to be the victim of her own vanity and the attentions of a man whose trade it is to flirt.

After a rapid and pleasant voyage, the steamer swept over the bar into the harbour of Alexandria, which was as pic-turesque as minarets, many pillared Pacha's houses, disabled three-deckers, and strange looking craft from the Greek islands, could make it. The passengers were landed in boats—some at the proper quay, where the usual crowd of filthy porters and hotel touters, surrounded them—others, amongst whom were Mrs. Chantney's party, were for some unknown

reason taken to the unfinished railway pier. They had to
hop over the great rough blocks of stone, entangled themselves in a wilderness of iron rails, and wondering why they
were there, found themselves at the back entrance of the
railway station. Here the officials in true Egyptian style,
seemed to know nothing of our travellers future, and to care
less. To add to the annoyance, strange to say for Egypt, it
began to rain in torrents. A leaky omnibus came to the aid
of our puzzled party, and off to an hotel was now the order
of the day. Here they found some of the passengers by the
Southampton steamer, amongst whom was Hampton, who
had been vainly enquiring for them in all directions. Laura
was delighted to see his bright handsome face once more.
He was very much sunburnt, had of course bought a blazing
red fez cap, and looked very Turkish indeed.

"Well, Laura," he said, "how do you like the journey?
I think it great fun. We had some strange characters on
board our ship; and I say, do you remember aunt Jane
talking of Mrs. Danvers. Well, she is here with her daughter
Fanny.

"Who is that little man staring at you so?" he whispered.

"Oh," she replied, with a smile, "that is a great friend of
ours, so romantic. I must introduce you to him. Monsieur
le Docteur, allow me to present my brother, an officer in the
Indian army."

The doctor was delighted at the notice taken of him, and
pulling Hampton into a corner informed him, that he was en-

chanted with the delightful English society he had met with,
and that Mrs. Chantney and Miss Templemore were *ravis-
santes*.

The usual bad breakfasts were eaten, and were followed
by a great deal of rushing about, consequent on false alarms
that the train was about to leave. After numerous delays,
all decidedly discreditable to the management of the P. and O.
company and the railway officials, the start really did take
place. This was a few years ago, and things are now better
managed; but were it not for the forgiving spirit produced
by the novelty, and by the anxiety to push on, in the case
of the outward bound passengers, and in that of the
homeward bound by their mad anxiety to reach England
on any terms, the want of order, smashing of boxes, trunks,
&c., and fine gentleman airs of some of the employés
(especially on the Indian side), would have brought any
company into disrepute. Passengers and their luggage
were literally shovelled in at one end of Egypt, jumbled up
well in the transit, and shot out at the other in the most
disgraceful way.

At Suez a long wooden slide was used to transfer the baggage from the steamer to the Arab boats or to the little steam-
tug. Down this we have seen go a general's cocked hat in a
tin case, followed at railway speed by a large wooden sea chest!
The fate of the cocked hat may be imagined. "Passengers
don't pay for the coals expended," used to be the dictum of
the ship's officers when talking on the above subject; but this

seems to have been rather an illusion, as the directors had to admit at one of their grand meetings to raise prices, that the poor belied passengers paid very well indeed. Properly printed orders ought to be given to every one, naming hours of delay at the different halts, and then there would be no confusion.

The Egyptian railway at Alexandria starts from an ill-built, trumpery station, through a low swampy country, the very picture of lower Bengal. Why the wretched villages are not wooded like those of the latter country, is strange, for they have the same rich soil and moisture. As to the huts or kennels of the fellahs, they are a disgrace to humanity; and rulers and ruled of such a land must be bad indeed—the one to allow such a state of things, the other to put up with it. It has well been said that Egypt is a land of soulless slaves governed by brigands.

Monsieur le Docteur managed to be in the same carriage with Laura, and was as devoted and romantic as ever. He had the volume of poems all ready, and she laughingly assented to his reading some of it to her; but the shaking of the railway carriage, with the originally tremulous, not to say impassioned, tones of the little man, produced such an effect that Mrs. Chantney had to beg him to leave off. Mr. Chantney did not generally laugh much, but he nearly went into a fit on this occasion. The little docteur, however, was so absorbed he took no offence, and said, "n'importe, he will do in the Red Sea."

After a very slow journey our travellers reached Cairo. It was nearly midnight, and a tremendous rush was made for the conveyances which take the passengers to the different hotels. Our friends failed in getting a carriage at once, and had to wait for some time. At last a phaeton and pair of Arab ponies were secured. They galloped to Shephard's, but were told every room was engaged. The same at the French hotel. They were starving. Where were they to sleep? A man who said he was a dragoman offered his services to find them a resting place, and installed himself on the carriage steps while he directed the coachman where to drive. They were, however, no more fortunate at the next place they drove to, nor the next, nor the next. The Arab coachman became thoroughly excited, and drove to imaginary hotels, simply for the purpose of running up his bill. At first Mrs. Chantney and party were highly amused at the frantic altercations between the coachman and the pretended dragoman (who spoke about ten words of English), but matters became serious when they found lights were being put out, and all honest people were going to bed. About this time they were joined by two men with lanterns, who seemed to know the dragoman. One of them got up beside the coachman, while the other took possession of the vacant carriage steps. The scene was supremely ridiculous. The new comers seemed to think that all the Arabic necessary to please English people with was the word "Buckshish," and this, at any rate, was all that was understandable in their horrible jargon.

Mr. Chantney's reply was, " Very well, you Cyclopean villains (one of them had lost an eye), take us to an hotel and I'll pay you anything."

A consultation would be held in Arabic, crack went the coachman's whip ; " Koobla," shouted the lanternmen and dragoman ; " Hurrah," cried Hampton, plunge went the ponies, and they drove up to another house. Still with the same result. Mr. Chantney here got into a towering passion, stood up on the seat, and made a long oration to his Arab friends. This only produced the usual reply from the dragoman, " I very good dragoman, plenty English got, give buckshish."

"Buckshish," screamed Mr. Chantney, " I'll buckshish you, you infernal Ishmaelites," and smashing one of the lanterns with a sweep of his stick, made a general onslaught on everybody.

This produced the unpleasant result of their being left without coachman, dragoman, or lanterns. He had, therefore, to take the reins himself, and drive back to Shephard's (followed at a respectful distance by the owner of the carriage), knocked that independent individual up, and insisted on sleeping in the coffee-room divan if nowhere else.

It now turned out that there were several reserved rooms to be had, but, in the usual Egyptian way of managing things, none of the hotel people had troubled themselves much about the matter. Had Mr. Chantney not forced his way into the house, his party might have slept in the streets.

The scarcity of the accommodation was caused by the homeward and outward bound passengers meeting together at

Cairo, the Pacha having, from some freak, forbidden the train
to go on to Alexandria for some hours. The apartments they
did secure were wretched. So, hungry, tired, and musquito
tormented, Laura passed the night in romantic Cairo. Next
morning some hundred people met to scramble for breakfast
in the well-known saloon ; and there being a few hours to spare,
the travellers afterwards scattered, some Pyramid-wards, and
some to the citadels, bazaars, &c. The scene before Shephard's at this time ought to have been sketched by John
Leech, and no one else. Twenty dirty, half naked, generally
(from ophthalmia) one-eyed Arab boys pushed twenty donkeys
and mules recklessly against one another. In broken English
they recommend their wretched steeds as " Handy Andy,"
" Greased Lightning," and a number of slang names, picked
up, goodness knows where,—one poor big-headed mule being
specially honoured by the name of the Duke of Wellington.
Add to these, twenty or thirty gentlemen, young and old, fat
and lean, competing for the possession of the above-mentioned
splendid stud—make them all smoking cigars, with muslin
pugrees round their heads, and cherry sticks for pipes in their
hands ; throw in fifty fearfully dirty porters, all shouting out
" Buckshish ;" make an outer circle of ten or fifteen antedi-
luvian flys (generally open phaetons) banging and crashing
their wheels together, and you have a faint idea of the confusion before the door of Shephard's hotel.

The railroad had not, at the period we write of, been
finished to Suez. Our travellers had, therefore, to undergo

the jolting and other miseries across the eighty miles of desert. There were the usual halts, breaks down, getting out of enthusiastic youths to look for agates in the once sea-washed stones of the wilderness, with all the little divertissements of that weary journey, culminating in the horrors of the now done-away-with Suez Hotel. Our friends were glad, indeed, when they found themselves on board the little tug which took them down the shallow bay, to the noble steamer (now, alas, a wreck!), the *Colombo*.

The overland trip to Suez is a mere party of pleasure ; but from this point people begin to talk seriously of the heat, and preparations for sleeping on deck are made by the more knowing travellers. The black crew and the punkahs seem strange, and speak of India to the uninitiated ; while the European officers, stewards and quartermasters look pale and delicate. As the steamer advances, the scenery on either side becomes of the most awfully impressive and melancholy-engendering character. The mountains, amongst which Sinai is conspicuous, frown down on the glassy sea, rugged, of a lurid black colour, and devoid of the slightest traces of vegetation. Treacherous coral reefs stretch from their base, and render the navigation most dangerous. The frightful deserts lying behind them may be pictured by the imagination, and the horrors of being wrecked in such an inhospitable region involuntarily force themselves on the mind. During some months the passage of the Red Sea is a perfect ordeal. Two stewardesses died of exhaustion a voyage or two before the one we record, and there is hardly any hot weather which does not see one or more of the passengers die of apoplexy. The hardiest natives of Bengal break down as stokers on board the steamers on this route; and the only race of human beings who can undertake the task, are the Seedees of Eastern Africa, and they are more like gorillas than human beings. To see one of these blue-black caricatures of humanity come up dripping from the stoke-hole, and throw himself on the hot iron plates round the funnel to cool himself, is enough to make one shudder. They are merry rascals, these poor Seedees, and Hampton and the other young men used to scream with laughter, at the indescribably ludicrous dance which they got up, under the stimulus of sixpences and shillings bestowed on them by the amused spectators. The natives of Bengal, who form the Lascar crew of the steamers, are a soulless, lazy set, and an African is worth a dozen of them.

In the voyage from Suez to Galle, lasting some sixteen or seventeen days, more harm is done to some constitutions than by a five years' residence in India; and there is little doubt that for the invalid the long sea voyage is the proper one, while it is also the best means for acclimatising the young Englishman to the tropics. From November to March the Red Sea is bearable, and our travellers were lucky enough to be in the best of these months, viz., December.

After two or three days everything and everybody settled into their proper places. According to promise, Laura's little friend, the doctor, daily regaled her with selections from the most romantic of the poems in his book. But though she understood French fairly, she could not thoroughly appreciate the subtle, not to say outrageous conceptions of the Gallic mind as portrayed in the pieces read to her; and notwithstanding all the tragical starts and exclamations of the enamoured Galen, we are afraid that the result, so far as inflaming her heart with a burning passion, was not encouraging. Truth, moreover, compels us to disclose the sad fact that, at last, when on deck (where everyone is all day), she saw him coming armed with the book as usual, she simulated (as a last resort) the most intense sleep, allowing her straw hat to fall on her dear little nose, and snoring quite audibly. This was very wrong, we admit, but it had the desired effect ; and when on approaching his divinity he used to find her asleep, he would raise both hands in admiration, whisper "quel ange," and softly steal away for fear of waking her.

As the steamer progressed on the journey southwards, windsails and punkahs helped to mitigate the heat, and great excitement was produced by the captain announcing that he would do his best to make Christmas day pass as merrily as possible.

Christmas day in the Red Sea! with the thermometer at 95° in the cabins! Not a sail on the water, or trace of living thing on the shore. Earthquake-riven mountains, the only representatives of old England's happy hills and dales. The prospect of years upon years of expatriation to many, and yet! mirth and laughter, dance and song. Verily the human mind is a wondrous work, and baffling to the analysis of the subtlest philosopher!

Plum pudding, mince pies, and all the other traditionary viands of the season, made their appearance in due course. Young ladies dressed their hair with extra care, and added a ribbon or two to their light muslin dresses. Young gentlemen engaged partners for the dance in the evening ; and the French docteur was nearly mad with the idea of his being able to show off his artistic steps " à la Français," Laura and even Mrs. Chantney having promised to dance with him. Some cynical and high-minded cadets wondered how people could be so mad as to dance in such a hot place, when they could have a pipe and a glass of grog under the foresail and be comparatively cool, but they were not much regarded, and were generally short and plain with red-haired tendencies.

There was no ship's band, but a young medical man on board played the concertina *à merveille,* one of the stewards performed very fairly on the violin, and another on the cornet, while Captain Desmond charmed every one (especially Miss Browning) by his delicious little romances, accompanying himself on the guitar. To increase the harmony, one of the newly married couples attempted, but signally broke down in a duet. The result of which catastrophe was, I am sorry to say, a total withdrawal of the lady's affections from her lord and master for nearly twenty-four hours.

Dancing, blue-lights, rockets, and punch in unlimited quantity, kept up the fun till late.

Monsieur le Docteur was highly pleased at the impression his Parisian steps had made, and was towards the end of the evening in a decidedly tragical and semi-tearful state. He said to Laura, "Mademoiselle, you have honoured me, your national enemy, by your consideration, I devote myself henceforth to your service, and pledge you in this glass of ponche." His hand went up! Bang! roared the unexpected report of a twelve-pounder fired to announce the end of Christmas day. The start caused the ponche to go the wrong way, and the doctor flew from the spot spluttering and maddened by the unfortunate interruption to his love making.

Next morning's sun shone on many a splitting headache, for oh that punch had been made with the horrible fire-water which the P. and O. directors call brandy, and the captain must have grinned a ghastly smile when he gave the order to the chief steward to "spare it not." Everything but the beer on the P. and O. steamers ought to be labelled poison, and wise the young beginner who limits his potations to that beverage. The table, too, on the Indian side is decidedly inferior. No one seems to look after anything; and the native "Jemmy Ducks" might be seen of a morning hauling out of the coops a dozen fowls and ducks which had died during the night, while half of those served up at table were saved from death by being killed. The fact is that European energy fails in the task of supervision, under the influence of intense heat, and the natives have it all their own way.

Having coasted past Mocha, celebrated for its coffee, the steamer fast approached that treeless, burnt-up heap of cinders, Aden; and all on board longed for a run on shore. Most of the gentlemen went to see the cantonments, which lie in the crater of an extinct volcano, and are well guarded from Arab incursions by its natural walls of rock. Hampton and the other young men had here their first look at a real live Sepoy, part of the garrison being from Bombay; and the former had also his first ride on a camel, which Albert Smith, we think, describes as being like sitting in a chair on the top of a hansom cab, on a bad road : his first attempt at mounting nearly broke his neck, for the brute rose suddenly, and he cut a somersault backwards. Cadets, however, have seven lives, and he escaped unhurt.

Aden is only interesting from its novelty and extreme ugliness, to which add clouds of insidious coal dust, and a burning sun, to render its charms complete. The Soomalies who come on board to sell coral and ostrich feathers, are certainly amusing for a time, as are also the divers who pick up sixpences; but the most welcome sound to the travellers is the order to "up anchor and away," from such a miserable place.

Eleven days of monotonous progress took the *Colombo* into the romantic harbour of Point de Galle.

Here was a contrast to the scene they had left behind them. Graceful cocoa palms bend their plumes over the sea,

every crevice in the rocks of the old Dutch fort grows something green; while on the other side of the bay the thickly
wooded hills rise higher and higher as they trend towards
the interior. At Aden it seldom rains; at Galle 'tis said they
have one shower at least a day, and although not healthy, it
is a sweetly romantic and picturesque spot. Here Hampton
wrote his second letter, which we transcribe for the benefit
of our readers:

" Point de Galle, Ceylon ;

January 3rd, 18—.

" My dear Jack,—My letter from Malta must have reached
you long ere this, and made you acquainted with my progress
Eastwards. We had very fine weather all the way to Alexandria, and I have nothing very striking to relate of that portion of my journey. Where do you think we found all the socks
which had been purloined ? Why, under the wash-hand stand,
where they were rolled into a rat's nest, and nearly chewed to
pieces. Binkey served the rat out rather cleverly one morning. He felt something running or dancing on the top of his
sheet, looked quietly up, and balancing his foot neatly kicked
Mr. Rat out of the port. Peace to his manes !

" That fellow in the Queen's has been giving me all sorts of
advice about India. He says an ensign can live very well on his
Indian pay, if he does not ape his seniors, and try to keep
horses and dogs, and go a-head. I'll be able to judge shortly
how far this is correct. Alexandria looks very picturesque from

the sea, but it is a wretched place when you leave the principal streets. All the lower classes, to speak *a la* Munchausen, have one eye (not in the middle of their forehead though). This is from ophthalmia, and a wretched sight it is, punning apart, to see the flies settling on a recent case. Mem. Bad place to send stereoscopes to. The flies in Egypt are perfectly regardless of *self*. You may kill them by fifties, they don't care. They only want some of *you*. I bought such a stunning fez for a smoking cap in a baazar, from an old image with a beard (of course, through an interpreter). I think he spat on the ground after he took the money. I wanted to know from the commissionaire, if he had done so, but that worthy was suddenly very deaf, and hustled me out of the place. Every look of a Turk is concentrated essence of insolence. Found my sister at one of the hotels, she looks older and more womanly already. It rained for hours in torrents, and some of the passengers who went sight seeing were thoroughly drenched. Saw any amount of wild ducks and ibis in the swamp skirting the railway, would have given something for a day's shooting. We had such a lark at Cairo, couldn't get bedrooms, and drove wildly through the streets half the night. Off to see the Pyramids next morning. They are certainly stupendous. Went on donkeys with some other fellows, rode one called Eclipse, such a brute. He lay down with me twice and tried to roll, but I was too quick for him. Coming home beat them all in a race.

" Had to go to Suez in vans, rail not being finished, terribly

cramping work. We were all glad to get on board the Indian
steamer.   Had a jolly row going down the Red Sea. It happened thus : One of the cadets would go up to the fore top.
While enjoying the view there, the chief mate saw him, gave
the wink to the lascars, and after a fearful struggle, in which
one man was nearly kicked overboard, some eight of them tied
him to the rigging.   Most of the military officers were highly
indignant at niggers being sent to tie up a white man, and
when the lascars came down a general onslaught was made.
To see fat little Major Smith, pitching into a thin lascar, all to
himself, was delicious. Matters, however, were rendered
serious by a mercantile traveller on board firing his revolver
either at or in the direction of a man in the rigging.   All the
stewards and European quartermasters mustered immediately
in the waist ; and in a little time there must have been a regular disturbance, but the captain put a stop to it by ordering
young Jones's release.   He came down, black as a sweep from
the soot, and his paroxysms of rage, in connection with his
begrimed face, were too much for any one's gravity.   He was
nicknamed Othello for the rest of the voyage.   Found the
benefit the other day for having studied under Herr Schacht.
Injured my watch in some way, and discovered a second class
passenger, a German, who could repair it.   He was delighted
to have some one who could talk *Deutsch* with him.

" We had great fun in the Red Sea on Christmas day.
Dancing, and all kinds of games.   You should have seen an
admirer of Laura's, a little Frenchman, with his head cocked

on one side, executing a regular *pas de ballet* in the quadrilles. A galvanised frog would have been astonished at his feats of agility. I am afraid he was very "much disguised" at last, for he was found weeping piteously at the foot of the funnel, at some ' malheur terrible ' which had happened to him. I danced with Fanny Danvers once, and took the opportunity of telling her that perfidy and woman were synonymous terms (this was after a lot of punch), and that I considered the Civil Service as the refuge of the ugliest men in England. We are nearly dead cuts now, and I hope the stinging of a remorseful conscience may harrow her soul, as the sensation novels say. By the bye, I nearly forgot to tell you that one of the newly-married couples, an indigo planter and his wife, fell into the Red Sea at Aden. As they were getting out of the boat which took them on shore, the Soomali boatman who held the bows of the rickety machine suddenly let go, and they were both pitched into the water. It was a sight to see the affectionate husband lift up his dripping wife, and carry her on shore. Haven't spoken a word to Fanny Danvers since Christmas day. She has completely fascinated that young civilian I wrote you about. He is ugly as sin, and such a muff! I have neglected to mention one great excitement which took place before we landed at Alexandria. It was on the occasion of the winning the lottery which is usually got up about the hour of arrival. The last few probable hours of dropping anchor are divided into quarters, or less, the lucky holder of the ticket specifying the exact time, winning the money. In this instance the sum was fifty pounds, and was won by a cadet. He is always betting, and will turn out a gambler or I'm mistaken. He bought the winning ticket from Binkey for fifteen shillings. We shall have another at the Sandheads. Hope I may win. The place I write from is charmingly romantic. Picture a tiny land-locked bay, water a deep blue, heaving in long smooth swells, till it breaks on the low sandy shore, which is clothed down to the very edge with the graceful cocoa-nut palm. On the left the storm-beaten rocks of the old Dutch forts challenge the breakers to come on ; and they *do* come, and are thrown up in snowy fragments into the air, sometimes even in calm weather, some twenty feet high. On the other side, steep and rugged rocks rise straight out of the sea, looking frowning and dangerous. Dot a dozen craft of all sizes here and there in the foreground, and you have the picturesque harbour of Galle. But you can not paint the constant roar, or the dashing spray, or the waves rolling to the foot of the palms, which bend over them lovingly.

" In haste, yours affectionately,
" HAMPTON TEMPLEMORE.

" P.S.—You should see my gold chain, which cost one rupee (two shillings). Everyone on board bought them. Of course they are not gold, but they do to hang keys on."

CHAPTER III.

MADRAS ROADS—CALCUTTA.

Before the passengers landed at Galle, to spend the hours of their stay, quite a scene had been got up in honour of the French Commandant, who, with Monsieur le Baron, here disembarked to join the China steamer. Everyone mustered at the gangway. " Vive l'Empereur !" and "Success to the Commandant !" was given by the gallant Major Mac-speechy, three hearty cheers made the air ring again, and the silence that followed was sweetly broken by a hundred voices joining in " Partant pour la Syrie." The effect was most impressive. The brave old soldier and his companion, deeply moved, stood hand on heart, and bowed their acknowledg-ments ; while the French docteur, and a French broker on board, rushed upon them and kissed them frantically. This rather spoiled the scene in English eyes ; but on the whole the parting compliment was a pretty one, and was duly appreci-ated by our Gallic friends, and their countrymen on board.

The "lions" at Galle are, a place called " Wauk Wallah," on the top of a hill, some four miles inland, and the Cinnamon Gardens. The former is a good specimen of tropical scenery,

being in the centre of wooded mountains, with a view of a
valley through which a river winds sluggishly along; but the
journey, from the steamer's limited stay, has generally
to be performed in the heat of the sun, which renders the
admiration of scenery rather a warm task.   The Cinnamon
Gardens have no special attraction.   Mrs. Chantney and
Laura preferred, therefore, being cool and comfortable in the
hotel, and soon had a host of Cingalese round them, offering
their different wares for sale.   Here is a cat's-eye stone, worth
two hundred pounds, and as big as a pigeon's egg ; or perhaps
they would like a sapphire, of which there were plenty, varying
from one to fifty pounds in price.   The gold work of Trichinopoly was temptingly displayed before them, mixed up with
beautiful tortoise-shell work-boxes, bracelets, combs, and
fifty other articles.   Papers full of small pearls, cinnamon
stones, Ceylon diamonds, moon stones, &c., could be bought
for a mere trifle; and how they sold the Trichinopoly chains,
looking exactly like gold, for two or three shillings, is a
marvel.   Laura was fascinated by a pair of exquisite fillagree
bracelets in gold, set with small but brilliant rubies, and after
a little bargaining Mrs. Chantney secured them for only
eight pounds.   Judges of precious stones can here buy jewellery
astonishingly cheap, but woe to those who know not the wares
of Birmingham, for it is a fact that some hundred pounds
worth of counterfeit trash is shipped monthly to this place.
A nice sapphire can be bought for ten pounds; and pearls
about half the size of a pea, are worth five shillings each.

After some twelve hours, the signal gun warned all stragglers
to wend their way on board; and 'mid a smart squall of wind
and rain, our voyagers steamed their way out of the romantic
but dangerous harbour of Galle.

Four days more and Laura would lose Mrs. Chantney. Her
thoughts now turned to her uncle, and the reception she would
meet at Calcutta. Would Mrs. Templemore be as kind as
her aunts in Cheltenham had been? Would she be pleased
with her, who had been brought up so simply? These and
kindred thoughts made her more and more anxious as she
approached her journey's end. Hampton cheered her up
every now and then, by saying she would have him to take
care of her; and when he was settled with his regiment, she
might live with him if she preferred it. But she could not
help having her forebodings, and felt miserable when the
anchor dropped at Madras, and she had to say good bye to
Mrs. Chantney, whose kindness throughout the journey she
had thoroughly appreciated. "I shall hear of your marriage
to some Grandee, soon," said that lady, "and I shall never
forgive you, if you do not write to me all about it. Good
bye," she said, with more emotion than Laura fancied her
capable of showing, "I have a strong affection for you, and
my parting warning is, never marry for wealth or position
alone."

A party of Madras friends here interposed, she and her
husband went through that truly gymnastic feat, getting into
a Masoolah boat, and Laura strained her eyes watching them,

till they were hidden by the big rollers which dash their snowy spray on that surf-beaten shore.

The little French docteur also landed. Poor little fellow, he was quite overcome. He came to say adieu.

"See," he said, "I have painted a likeness of you. I shall wear it next my heart. Accept this little souvenir ('twas the book of poems), and when you are happy in other scenes, think sometimes of the poor desolate Achille Moran."

He rushed away, sprang too hastily into the Masoolah boat (which was very large and deep), was caught by a thwart, and the last Laura saw of him, as a heavy swell swept the boat away, was the poor little docteur's heels stuck up in the air. As she sat pensively looking over the side, she heard a voice behind her say ('twas Captain Desmond), "You seem to feel Mrs. Chantney's loss very much, Miss Templemore. You ought not to give way to grief, but think of the gay scenes awaiting you in Calcutta; I am only afraid that those who have had the pleasure of your society on board, will not be able to vie with the high and mighty ones you will meet there. I trust, however, you will not totally forget us when you land."

Laura was glad to hear any sympathising voice, and spoke more kindly to him than she was wont, and he was more constantly by her side.

Hampton was delighted with the novelties around him. "Look here," he said, "Laura, there's a catamaran with ever so many queer looking fish in a basket; that fellow must have a nice idea of balancing to be able to poise himself on

those two logs; and, by Jove, there's a lot of plantains
and other strange looking Indian fruit. I must go and get
some."

Had it not been for the heat, the constant rolling motion
(the chronic disease of the Madras roads), and the glare,
the different groups on board the steamer at this time
would have been highly amusing. Here are half-a-dozen
men with enormous turbans, balancing, carefully, high-
heaped glasses of suspicious looking ices. The look of
melancholy on the poor fellows' faces, as they see the coloured
delicacy fading gently away, while your lordship will not
look round and buy, is highly ludicrous. Have they any
consciences, these ice-men? If they have, would they allow
the thirsty griffs on board to eat half-a-dozen, nay a dozen of
their concentrated essence of cramp?

A party of snake charmers helped to wile away the weary
hours; and the ladies were enchanted by the beautifully worked
muslins, some of them embroidered with beetles' wings, for
which Madras is famous.

At last the cargo is landed, some of the gentlemen who
have spent the day at the far-famed club on shore, return at
the last moment; the mail arrives, and once more the land is
left behind.

On the fourth evening a blue light suddenly warns the
passengers they are in pilot's-ground. It is answered, and
after a short interval, the graceful pilot brig sweeps alongside,
and sends that astonishingly "got up" individual, a Bengal

Pilot, on board; and hearts beat high to think that to-morrow the curtain will rise on their first day's Indian experience. To-morrow the husband will clasp the dear wife in his arms, who has been rescued from death, perhaps, by her trip to Europe; children will meet parents whom they have forgotten; yes, totally forgotten. To-morrow the engaged one will charm the eyes of her expectant lover. To-morrow will enchanting portraits of lovely maidens be compared with the present originals, and woe, is me, what a demolishing there will be of long cherished fancies. Julia will be found to be short and dumpy, while Hetty's golden hair turns out to be red! To-morrow will all the batchelorhood of Calcutta, who can slip away from their desks, be on the deck of the steamer, scrutinising the beauties of its fair freight, and may be a marriage or two will there and then be concocted in the brains of some hitherto unconquered swains.

By daylight the low flat shores of the estuary of the Hooghly are distinctly visible. They have been often described in anything but flattering terms, and certainly a more uninteresting, desolate scene, never disappointed expectant traveller. The muddy waters of the river roll down between a vast region of deadly swamps, bearing on their polluted surface the constantly recurring dead bodies of the pretendedly, but not in this instance certainly, fastidious Hindu. The land seems scarcely above the high tide level, and is one unbroken flat for hundreds of miles, while the large forest trees on the shores having all been cut down, there is nothing for the eye to rest on but an endless succession of low brushwood and marsh. It is indeed a horrible spot.

If you are ever anchored off Sangor of a moonlight night, look over the side of your craft, and wonderingly watch the phosphorescent water, broken into fiery eddies as it swirls past the cable, which is creeping and surging out its acknowledgment of the power of the mighty tide.

See the snake-like Medusæ become lighted up as they are twisted about in the lambent flood. Then, with a splash, throw in your hooks, baited with almost anything, and shudder as you hear the monster sharks come rippling up to see what is astir, leaving long streams of light behind them. Ugh! it makes one's flesh creep to think of falling overboard in such a place. Harken to the jackal's mournful scream as it is wafted faintly from the shore; know that on all sides the low marshy forests breed the deadly fever, which, borne on the dew-laden night wind, may haply be laying its clammy hands on you, and then, like Mark Tapley in Eden, acknowledge that it is creditable to be jolly in such a place.

The banks of the river gradually become more interesting as Calcutta is approached; but when it is borne in mind that that badly chosen capital is only eight feet above ordinary flood tides, it will easily be understood that the adjacent country, which is still lower, cannot have many charms. In fact, it is only the strip of wooded villages on either side of the river which hides the deformities lying behind, giving that picturesque look to the banks so much admired by the enthusiastic but uninitiated voyager.

The last vista off Garden Reach revealing the mass of shipping, strange native craft, and white-washed houses of the aristocratic quarter of the town is decidedly fine, especially when seen on a bright cold-weather day.

Now comes the excitement of landing. The telegraph and the heavy gun from the fort have warned all Calcutta that the steamer has passed a place called Atchipore, and expectant friends and relatives hurry down to the Ghants or landing-places, and secure Bhauliahs and dingies to take them on board, before the anchor is fairly down.

"I wonder which is uncle George," said Hampton to his sister, as they watched the little fleet struggling up against the tide. "How anxious I feel. I wonder if he is like what papa was."

Laura hoped that the tall, stout gentleman in that gay, well-manned, green painted boat may be he ; and true enough it is.

"Templemore? Oh, yes, there they are," said somebody, and suddenly Laura was in the embrace of her uncle.

"Well, Hampton, my boy," he said cheerily. "Why what a great fellow you are! Six feet, or I'm mistaken. And, bless me, how like your poor father. Had a pleasant voyage? Haven't given your heart into anyone's keeping, Laura, have you? No, that's right. We must keep that article labelled ' fresh as imported,' yet awhile. Come along,

I'll take you on shore at once, and leave a chuprassee (orderly)
to look after your things. Your aunt is in the garry (carriage)
waiting for you."

A few strokes of the oars, a jump on shore, Laura steps
into a handsome barouche, and is welcomed by Mrs. Templemore, who then shook Hampton by the hand in a cold and
languid way, complained of being kept so long in the sun,
and made a sign to the gaily dressed syces to tell the coachman to drive home.

The mettled Arabs sprung to the whip, and they were
soon rolling along towards one of the suburbs, in which
George Templemore resided. His present appointment was
in connection with the district surrounding Calcutta, called
" The Twenty-four Pergunnahs," and he might almost be
considered a resident of the town, although a district
official.

Laura had time to notice that her aunt was a pale, delicate
woman, who had once been pretty, and doubtless thought
herself so now. She was dressed in that light semi-French
toilet peculiar to the rich of India, and everything she wore
was superbly good and elegant. She scrutinised the new
comers, and on the whole seemed rather satisfied.

" We must get you some nice light things suited to the
climate," she said, to Laura, " and you must lose that horrid
sunburnt colour before I take you to Government House."

She seemed to look upon Hampton, and all cadets, as
something to be endured, and that young gentleman grew as

nice a little crop of dislikes to her, on the spot, as any malicious fairy could have wished.

"Fancy her confounding me with such fellows as that vulgar little snob, Binkey," he said to Laura, afterwards, "she is a mass of affectation, and, hang me, if I like her."

They were not long in driving through the handsome entrance gates of Laura's future home, and as it was similar to most of the houses of the same class, near Calcutta, we shall describe it.

As the visitor left the dusty road and swept past the lodges at the gate, his eye was first caught by the glassy waters of a square tank, about a couple of acres in extent. Beyond this, a magnificent banyan tree was the most conspicuous object. Then there were three or four snow-white, diminutive native cows, with a dozen beautifully-marked (Jumna Paree) goats, feeding on the twenty or thirty acres of closely cropped grass. Here and there clumps of bamboos threw up their feathery stems, while the thick dark green mango vied in beauty with the teak, sisso, and other forest trees dotted about. Plots of flowers filled the foreground of the approach, and here is the house. It is white as alabaster, with green Venetian doors and windows. Fluted pillars support noble verandahs on the ground and first floors. A massive portico covers the carriage way. The rooms are thirty or forty feet long and twenty feet high. On the ground floor they are paved with checquered marble. Gilded punkas swing in each room, ornamented with stencilling to agree with the walls. Vases, costly furniture, and a statuette or two, complete the luxurious elegance of the rooms. Half a dozen native servants in snow-white robes and coloured girdles, glide bare-foot here and there. The Hooghly, half a mile or more wide, covered with imaginable and unimaginable native boats, flows swiftly past. Picture this, and you have some idea of the rich civilian's residence in Bengal.

Laura was enchanted with her own room, into which her aunt led her, and it would have been hard to say which was the prettier, of its kind, the room or its future occupant. It looked out on the river. From its lofty beams hung a green and gold punka. The walls were pure white with a light stencilled pattern in green, the cool shining mats were relieved here and there by bright-coloured Mirzapore rugs. The furniture was comparatively scanty, for coolness is the great desideratum in an Eastern bedroom, but it was of beautiful design and of solid mahogany. A cheval glass, wardrobe, spring sofa, that peculiarly Indian institution a snow-white musquito tent, enclosing within its transparent walls an elegantly-shaped sleeping couch, a few bright green bows of ribbon here and there, a vase or two of flowers, two native women in their graceful garb, ready to answer the faintest call, and our description is complete.

Hampton reported himself next morning to the proper officials, and was duly allotted quarters in the fort, which said quarters consisted of two rooms opening, as did some fifty others, out of a broad corridor, running through the cadets' barrack.

The contrast between his uncle's beautiful country house and *his* bare, shabby chambers, struck him rather forcibly, and led him to meditate on the different points of view, which life may be contemplated from, and to wish that he had studied hard enough for the Artillery or Engineers. I will work well now, he thought, and why should I not achieve what others have ? That day made a wonderful change in our hero and influenced his future as much as the journey out did that of his sister. He was more and more surprised to see the boyish and unthinking pranks, played by some of the youngsters domiciled with him, and his thoughts recurred to his friend on board, who had warned him as to the opinion generally held of cadets.

There is no doubt that at the time we write of (and probably it is so now), Calcutta was, without exception, the worst city in the world to let inexperienced boys loose in, and it would have been well if Government had long ago devised some means to keep their young protogés amused and employed. Amusement there is none in the City of Palaces, the rich European and Eurasian community being too small to keep up any places of public resort, and in fact the climate for eight months is so oppressive, that no one cares to go out oftener than can be avoided. To sit out theatrical entertainments in which the dripping actors are only one shade more pitiable than the parboiled audience, is a feat only attempted.

by the uninitiated. And when it turns out that the evaporation of vital moisture, has been replaced behind the scenes by champagne during the last two acts, the result may be imagined. A beautiful theatre was built some twenty-five years ago, an English company was imported, and every one got up an enthusiasm, but it only lasted some two or three years. Death and drink finished many of the actors, and the respectable portion of the audience gradually melted away.

Dinner parties are given in the hot weather, but they break up early, and are looked on as unavoidable inflictions.

The private billiard tables of particular regiments, and those at the two great clubs are practically shut to the young beginner, and the racket court and cricket club, are in the same category, from the expense attendant on them. Of course the new arrivals from England are under military discipline whilst in barracks, and are so far kept in check, but they have no means afforded them of wiling away pleasantly the tedious hours of an Indian day or night, and the result is that out of barracks, they are to be found in the town, in which the billiard rooms are disreputable, and where, besides billiard rooms, there is not a place in which a young man can find amusement. During the cold months certainly, a strolling company of niggers, a concert singer, or a circus may make their appearance, but they are generally fifteenth rate, and you cannot go every night to hear the same thing.

Add to this doleful state of matters the temptation to drink from the great heat, the want of any small parties or reunions, where the young men might spend an evening among ladies, and then wonder that they turn out so well as they do. To those who have no friends or relatives the situation is, of course, worse. No one warns them against the deadly effects of shooting in the sun, late hours, and to get the steam up, the consequent peg (brandy and water) in the morning. The result is, that a boy's constitution gets a severe shake before he has been a year in the country. We may have Utopian ideas on the subject, but we think that a club for cadets, under proper supervision, supported principally by Government, with a gymnasium, racket court, library, reading and billiard rooms, &c., might have been instituted with the best results. As Hampton Templemore's promised letter to his friend in Cheltenham illustrates the subject we have been writing on, we here give it.

"Fort William, Calcutta;

January, 185—.

"My dear Jack,—I now fulfil the promise I made in my Ceylon letter.—Light breezes and a summer sea prevailed all the way from Galle to Madras, at which place we left our friends, Mr. and Mrs. Chantney. Whoever first conceived Madras must have had queer notions of a safe anchorage, and of a site for a capital. A tremendous current runs past the place, and the surf beats more or less on the beach, ac-

cording to the humour it may be in—nothing but the Massoolah boats and the catamarans can live in it. The former
are large and curiously-shaped (very like the last new life
boats; by the bye, whose was the first idea, eh?), not nailed
together, but sewn with rattan, and they leak like sieves;
but they are elastic. One of them rose to a sea, dashed
against the bottom of our gangway ladder, had a thwart
bodily torn out, and was not a bit the worse. An English boat
would have been in two pieces. The catamarans are two light
logs, lashed together, and pointed at one end; they are always
under water a little, and the feet of the men on board are
like a washerwoman's hands, from being constantly wet.
I wonder the sharks don't stop the catamaran business—they
say that there are lots in the surf (ground ones), and that a
white man is lost if he is in the water any time. A little
Frenchman we had on board had such a spill into a Massoolah
boat; he jumped down at the wrong time—the boat jumped
up—they met—and the next moment nothing was to be seen
but a pair of heels in the air. Would you believe it? the
sporting cadet bought the lucky ticket, and won the lottery
again—I mean the one at the Sandheads. The entrance to
the Hooghly is very disappointing, as every one knows. The
scenery is better nearer Calcutta, and the first view of the
town is very fine. I am now in the Cadets' Barracks. I
could have lived at my uncle's for some time, but I prefer
being independent. He has a beautiful place up the river.
They call it cold weather just now, but at mid-day it is very

hot. Some of my chums have been out snipe shooting in the salt lakes, and two of them are already laid up with fever. There has been a terrible fracas amongst the cadets, in which, thank goodness, I had no hand. One young fool quarrelled with another—called him out. They had only one pistol—this they loaded with nails, went on the flat roof of the barracks, cast lots for the weapon, and the one who got it, shot the other in the leg—literally nailed him. They were both nearly cashiered, but they got off on account of their youth, and the fairness displayed in their ridiculous duel. I am determined not to associate with any fellow who acts like a schoolboy, and am therefore rather disliked. The quantity of Pariah dogs, with clipped ears and tails, that have been bought by the griffs as terriers, would form a pack. Of course the moment they are taken outside the fort and set on anything, they bolt the other way, and are soon with their old masters the mehters; so we shall get rid of them in time.

"Talking of dogs, I was witness yesterday of the most extraordinary 'dodge' for catching jackals that can possibly be imagined. A native Shikaree (hunter), who supplies the Tiretta Bazaar here with live animals, which he sells to the numerous dog-keeping community, offered to take a young fellow I know, who is in a merchant's office in the town, to the scene of action, and I was asked to accompany them. Before day-break we met at the river side—crossed over to a place called Howrah, and walked smartly on for about two miles, till we came to a likely spot. This was a glade in a

thickly wooded part of one of the numerous villages which
line the Hooghly's banks. Our guide ensconced young Burton
and myself behind some bushes on one side of this glade, and
commenced operations.

"The actors were the man and a little boy armed with a short
stick.　The former began by covering about half an acre of
the field thickly over with tough nooses, pegged tightly into
the ground.　This done, he went into ambush with his assistant, and presently we heard the most extraordinary scuffling
noise, as if an old dry hide was being knocked about, while
lugubrious and heart-rending cries, as if from some billy-goat
who was being led to the slaughter or otherwise most shame-
fully illtreated, rent the air.　This lasted a minute or so, and
we strained our eyes to see what would come next.　Burton
gave me an awful pinch on the arm, which I forgave when I
saw his reason for inflicting it.　There, on the opposite side of
the vista, was a fine large male jackal, peeping out with cocked
ears, and evidently wondering what goat was being massacred,
by whom, and why should not he share, &c.　He looked round
—'All right—there's nobody in sight, I'll just slink over to
the side the noise comes from.'　Stealthily, with tail down, he
glides over.　Hurrah! he's in the middle of the snares and
tumbling head over heels.　Quick as the leopard in his spring,
out jumps the little boy, bang! crack! the jackal has two
sounding taps on the back of his head.　Out whipcord, tie
up his mouth, ditto his four legs, shoulder arms, and number
one is bagged as quickly and quietly as you please.　We re-

peated this half a dozen times and ended in having three old
jackals and a cub. The implements of the shikaree's trade on
this occasion (for they have a hundred other manœuvres) were
an old goat skin, and something which he put in his mouth
when he imitated the dying goat.

"Another cashiering business nearly came off about a week
ago. A party of youngsters from the Fort got into a disreputable row with some sailors in a low part of the town; the
whole of them were put into Chokey (the police-station), and
it was only from the consideration of the magistrate that they
were let off so easily. I hear that I am likely to be posted to
a regiment at Allahabad, and glad shall I be when I get out
of this place. Fort William is healthy enough, but one of the
guard houses at the Water Gate is notoriously bad, eleven
men out of the Sepoy guard were struck down by cholera, one
night, last hot weather. If young officers expose themselves
unnecessarily in the sun, keep late hours, drink and smoke too
much, what shall I say of the poor European soldiers. Uneducated, without a single aid to keep them amused or employed
they lie drunk and helpless about the bazaars, and are the
scorn of every passing native. It is disgraceful the way they
are neglected. They may be 'such desperate scoundrels,' as
a Queen's officer called them, the other day to me, but I don't
believe it, and they are the holders of this empire. If every
European soldier were treated like a gentleman, housed and
fed properly, and engaged to serve only for seven years, I
verily believe it would be cheaper in the end than the present

system is. Regiments think nothing of losing ten or fifteen per cent. the first year.

"My uncle George says that the amount of injury done to our rule by the scandalous conduct of the lower classes of Europeans is barely balanced by the knowledge the natives have gained, of their indomitable pluck.

"I have been round the suburbs lately on horseback. Such a dreadful conglomeration of muddy swamps, filthy native villages, picturesque tanks, temples, and gaudily ornamented houses, can hardly be conceived. Were the natives not vegetarians, the refuse from their houses would render their villages uninhabitable, but as it is, when the cholera does break out they are swept away in hundreds. Only a mile or less from the aristocratic quarter of the town, and *that* on the side from which the South-east monsoon blows, the land shelves down to a level with horrible low salt swamps, which extend for hundreds of miles, east and west. How Calcutta is as healthy as it is, is wonderful. It must proceed from the height at which Europeans sleep from the ground, and from the marshes at the back of it being salt, and under the influence of heavy tides. Were they composed of stagnant fresh water, Calcutta would be untenable. I must now close this letter. I trust that the next mail will bring me one from you, with all the Cheltenham news, and with kindest regards,

"I am, yours affectionately,

"HAMPTON TEMPLEMORE."

CHAPTER IV.

THE BAZAAR—AN INDIAN NIGHT—MRS. BLANDON'S "AT
HOME."

Mrs. Templemore's mansion was a favorite resort of the
civil and military loungers of Calcutta, and the two great
military stations of Barrackpore and Dumdum. The fame of
Laura's beauty added, of course, to the stream of visitors, and
her aunt was enchanted at the *éclât* created by her arrival.
One day, as they were sitting working some elegant trifles,
the noise of buggy-wheels announced a visitor, whose card
was brought in by the attendant chuprassee. The room was
very much darkened, or Mrs. Templemore would have noticed
a slight flush on Laura's face when she replied to her inquiry,
as to whether she knew the gentleman.

"Oh yes,—Captain Desmond. He came out with us."

Before she could say more he was ushered in. Mrs. Templemore was charmed with her visitor, and her practised eye
soon saw that he admired Laura. Oh, oh, she thought after
he left, here is conquest number one, and I am very glad of
it, for my own girls will be coming to India in two years, and
I cannot afford to have them cut out by this pretty niece of
mine.

"How do you like him, Laura ?" she said.

"Oh, very well, but—"

"But what ? He is handsome, accomplished, and will soon be a major. I begin to think you are very fastidious."

This was said in a very sharp, heartless way, and Laura felt that her trials had commenced. Her mother would not have talked to her so. The tears came to her eyes but she struggled hard, and replied pretty firmly that she did not like his manner to ladies. "He speaks so confidently, and then he flirted with a young lady on board, Miss Browning, to whom I have taken a dislike."

"Oh, is that all ; a little jealousy, I see. You'll get over that by and bye, when you have seen more of him. I shall ask him to dinner next week."

That evening Mrs. Templemore took Laura to the Rotten Row of Calcutta, called the Strand, on the banks of the river. To the new comer the concourse of vehicles, some of them containing gorgeously dressed natives, the fleet of first-class ships, picturesquely dispersed over the broad surface of the Hooghly, the massive fort, the pleasure grounds, named the garden of Eden, from having been planted by Lord Auckland's sisters, and the semicircle of palatial buildings in the back ground, make up a charming picture. When bright moonlight and sweet music are added to the scene, it is no wonder that the soft whisperings of love, or maybe, flattery, seem doubly irresistible to the fair inmates of the carriages, gathered in groups round the band, to whom all is so like fairy land.

Laura pointed out Miss Browning as well as some of her other shipmates. The former was riding a handsome chestnut Arab, and had already gathered a group of followers round her.

"So that is your rival, Laura," said her aunt, "she is a handsome woman, but has no chance with you, at least with men like Captain Desmond. See, they are all boys who are riding with her."

She was right, Desmond did prefer Laura, and had been watching for her carriage for some time. He came up as they stopped at the band.

"What think you of Calcutta by moonlight, Miss Templemore, charming—is it not ? Il Balen sounds sweetly mid the din of the native town, and the hum of the tide as it sweeps up this huge river. How does it affect you, to gladness or sorrow ? As for me, I feel alone and miserable in this strange land."

Laura had been thinking of her English home, and required little to make her share in Captain Desmond's melancholy.

"I quite agree with you," she said, "in feeling sad, *so sad*, but then that is for us women, you know, your role is to mount your milkwhite steed, and attack all griffins, giants, and chimeras dire, which may cross your path, including the demon melancholy."

He sighed and said no more. Mrs. Templemore asked him if he knew many people in town. He said " no, he had called everywhere, but there seemed a want of real sociability."

"Then I have just the thing to cure your ennui." Here is

one of my friend Mrs. Blandon's invitation cards, which I
am at liberty to give to you. It is rather too dark for you to
read it just now, but it is to say that her house is open twice a
week for all who are in her set; you will find it the only place
in Calcutta where you can pass an evening pleasantly. There
is no formality :you may come or go when you like, and the
society is delightful, I hope to meet you there to-morrow
evening." He seemed delighted at the prospect, said "good
night," and rode slowly away.

The ladies fell back in their seats, and in silence the pre-
scribed number of rounds of the drive were made, and the
usual recognition of friends took place, till the sharp night air
and sudden darkness following closely on the short twilight
warned them homewards.

The horses and syces (grooms who run by the carriage)
seemed to feel the excitement of a return to their dinners, and
to be glad to leave the monotony of the course. The coachman gave his whip an extra artistical sweep over his horses,
and with many a bound and spring the fiery Arabs rattled
their light freight up the fine road leading from the river.

Laura having expressed a strong desire to see the native
bazaars, her aunt ordered the coachman to drive through some
of them, much to our heroine's gratification and amusement.
Everything was bewilderingly strange, and suggestive of the
fairy Eastern tales so dearly loved in youth. Night favoured
the illusion. The roads were narrow, and studded continu-
ously with booths or shops all open in front without door or

window. The alternations from light to shade were startling, for out of the European portion of the town, the street lamps are few and far between. A sudden glare momentarily revealed a group of figures working at their trade, and then would come an interval of intense darkness. Now a long-continued series of lighted shops makes everything around visible.

That circle of clean dressed, white coated, and skull capped Mahomedans, is composed of muslin embroiderers; wonderful is the work they produce, and so cheap. A splendidly worked handkerchief could once be bought for two rupees or four shillings, and every other article of dress in proportion. But prices are now changed. Here is a confectioner's resplendent with coloured lanterns, which show off to perfection the snowy piles of tinsel-covered sweatmeats, or hissing pans filled with the dearly loved (to the native) curly jullaybee like vermicelli in shape, and composed of flour, butter, sugar, and spices, or the awfully luscious ludoo, made from curds, sugar, cardimums, &c. Look at the display made by his neighbour, the shoemaker, red shoes, with heels, yellow slippers without them, blue or green ones to suit some tastes, uncoloured ones to please others, gold embroidered ones if you like, or silver ditto, you have only to walk in, and you must be satisfied.

Who is that, sitting monkey like on his board, smoking abstractedly, and gazing on vacancy? 'Tis the oil vendor, who is patiently waiting for some one to come for half-a-farthing's worth, which he will ladle out with a little scoop,

made of a dwarf cocoanut shell, while his measure is a piece
of the same kind of nut, with a hole in the bottom. This is
stopped up with a finger of his left hand, which he will with-
draw when it is full, and the liqu'd can be skilfully guided
into any receptacle.

That man, bearded like the pard, is a retainer of some rich
Rajah or Baboo, we mean the one sitting in the armourer's
shop, there, chaffering about the price of that murderous looking sword : around the booth are hung shields and spears, and
all the strange implements of native warfare.

Now is passed that fascination of all fascinations a cloth
shop, or native linendrapers, hung with the bright colours
which the native revels in.   Chintzes red, and chintzes blue,
tastefully relieved by snowy long cloths or striped muslin
wares, making the place gay beyond description, and the result
you see is a crowd always hanging about the enchanting spot.

In the next a money changer sits statue-like behind his
heaps of gold and silver, beside him a silver hookah shines in
the rays of light thrown on it by a quaintly fashioned brazen
lamp, resting in a niche of the wall, while a faint smoke
curls up from its glowing chillum (bowl), scenting the air
with incense-like perfume.

The background is occupied by a massive wooden treasure-
chest on low wheels, which opens from the top, and on which
at night sleeps either the money-changer himself or some
trusty relative. It is a curiously, carved, unwieldy old affair,
and is rendered doubly secure (in its master's eyes) by being

daubed over with vermilion sketches of some favorite deity, and beautified after a native's ideas of beauty by patches of tinsel stuck on here and there.

A dismal cave is this abode of Mammon and the imperturbable Shylock who presides over its shining heaps is a fitting occupant of its mysterious gloom. He never smiles. His profits are generally small, but he is frugal and patient—so patient. His penury extends to his household, and with his own hands he weighs out twice a day with unflinching exactness the miserable portion of rice and lentils to his women and children, which forms their dinner and supper. At last, after a long series of years he counts his hoard by the lac (100,000 rupees), and then, instead of a baronetcy, or a villa at Twickenham, or Peers for his sons-in-law, he suddenly becomes religiously mad, covers himself with sackcloth and ashes, feasts every Brahmin he can induce to come to his entertainments, settles the most of his money on his nearest of kin, and wanders away on some tedious pilgrimage, to be choked to death, perhaps, on the cold bank of some sacred river, or to have his funereal obsequies performed by the vulture and the jackal after he has sunk down to die by some lone jungle-side. This is no exaggeration, and conscience, which maketh cowards of us all, thus drags to his dismal fate the rapacious, cruel, never-relenting usurer of usurers, the Bengalee money-changer.

Ah! what have we here? it must be Alladin's palace in very deed. No! after all it is only a gold lace and tinsel maker's with all his gaudy wares, whirling and shimmering before his cunningly arranged lamps.

Next to this gay place, looming through the smoky atmosphere, without a light to relieve its gloomy vastness, is a convent like pile, a rich native's house, girt round by lofty walls, round which is huddled a nest of squalid huts.

Now they are in the crush again, and oh dear! have so nearly run over that woman, who with a little child seated monkey-like on her hips, would waddle across the road. They always do so, just before the horses' noses, these native women.

As the carriage moves slowly along the eye rests on the painted fukeer prowling about for alms, the sleek, half-naked Hindu, or the patriarchally bearded Mussulman. What a living miscellany! There goes a long tailed Chinese in his clean nankin shirt and trowsers, followed by a mob of hideous African sailors from the Arab ships. See how gracefully those Hindu women balance their heavy water pots on their heads. They have to thread their way past those bullock carts, which come "wobbling" along rendering the night hideous with their screaming wheels, and nearly stopping up the road. It is a wonder some of them do not drop their precious freight of tank water, in the confusion, but they do not, and disappear down one of the dusty gullies to their mat and mud built huts in the background.

Samneywallah Beyt (literally, sit down in front there) shout the syces running on each side the horses. Clouds of dust arise. Phew! there's a pungent smell from a drug vendor's, followed by a sweet smell from a perfumer's, then a hundred other smells, some of them overpoweringly bad. Here is a musical procession, the drums and fifes making the horses nearly go mad, while the din is augmented by the gongs of yonder temple. Dust! smells! drums! distraction, who can ever forget thee, oh, Calcutta Bazaar!

The road became clearer of obstructions, and the horribly medicated taste of the bazaar air began to subside as they reached the suburbs and were whirled into the clear air on the banks of the river, while the stars shone out brightly, and the young moon's rays showed the snow white mansion of Mr. Templemore in all its beauty.

Hampton, who is to dine with his uncle to-day, is ready to hand the ladies out of the carriage, and heartily joins in Laura's condemnation of the native town.

" What nonsense people do get into their heads in England," he sagely remarked, " about orientalism generally." The fact is that Asiatics seem constitutionally wanting in those finer perceptions which lead to the refinements of civilised European life.

As Hampton led his aunt into the house, he informed her that he had secured the week's leave she had suggested to him, and that he was her humble slave to command for that time. Laura was so glad to have him with her for a whole week, and she tripped lightly up to her room, surprising the sedate native ayahs by gallopading the last few steps as she entered it. Neither of the orphans felt at ease with their aunt,

and they instinctively clung to each other and to their uncle,
who showed his fondness for them, while his wife seemed at
the best but lukewarm in her affection.

"Well Hampton, my boy, how do you like India?" said
his uncle as they sat after dinner by themselves. "You have
your own way to work up, and if you take my advice you
will study hard and pass for interpreter as soon as possible.
You know that the money your poor father left has been
nearly all expended in your education, and you and Laura have
only about a thousand pounds each left, but this ought to
keep you out of debt, and purchase any steps, when you are
posted to your regiment."

Hampton thanked his uncle for all his kindness, said he had
made up his mind to follow his good advice as to studying,
and made him laugh at some of the doings of the young men
in the fort.

"I wonder how those gaunt, soldier-like Sepoys have any
respect at all for the boys put in command over them," said
his uncle, "especially when they are as insolent as they can
be to the men. I'll tell you what it is, there will be a terrible
blow up, some day. The present generation of natives have
out-lived the memory of the conquest of Bengal, and, with the
usual vanity of Asiatics, think they are, in everything but
mechanical genius, the superior of the white man. They are
so far right that, although not so fleshy, the up-country native
will compete in athletic exercise with any European. How
many of the officers or soldiers you have seen in the fort could

wrestle with those lean, wiry, Sepoys? Perhaps for a spurt the European would be stronger, but in five minutes the wonderful wind and endurance of the vegetarian versus the meat-eater would be seen. Fifty out of a hundred of those fellows would get up to-morrow morning, walk their sixty miles, and eat their dinners as usual. And they would do this for a week. Individually, too, I am certain that the men of a Sepoy regiment would generally have no objection to meet any European in single combat with swords."

"Then what are they wanting in?" asked Hampton.

"I can hardly describe it," said his uncle; "but I think it is their want of confidence in each other which makes them fight badly in bodies, and last of all European bravery, which is a total abnegation of self (in which all calculation is thrown aside) a burning madness of the brain, is never reached by the native of India, except, perhaps, when he is drugged, and that, after all, is artificial; while in the white man the phrenzy is instinctive, God-given."

After listening to his uncle's invaluable hints on his future conduct Hampton changed the subject to sporting. George Templemore had been one of the best riders and hog hunters of his day, and Hampton could have listened to him for hours as he recounted his hair breadth escapes.

"By the bye," said he, "if you would like to see some sport I can give you a letter of introduction to a planter friend of mine, Mr. Besborough, who writes me that they are going to get up a meeting next week."

Hampton eagerly accepted the offer and it was arranged that he should leave for Kishnaghur, by Palankeen Dawk, that day week. They now joined the ladies. Hampton noticed that his sister looked triste, and drawing her into the verandah, asked her the reason.

"Hampton dear," she said, "you are independent, look at me, when our money is all gone what is my future; and, do you know, I fear my aunt may persuade me into some marriage I do not like."

Hampton was all indignation. "If she tries to do so," he said, "come to me, we may be poor but we shall at least be independent. Besides, I am sure uncle George will never allow you to be sacrificed to the caprice of his heartless wife."

Laura felt a little reassured, and they re-entered the drawing-room. The conversation now turned on Mrs. Blandon's "at home," and the next Government House Ball and Mrs. Templemore was soon deep in the mysteries of tulle, lace, wreaths, and feathers.

Early hours are kept in India. Ten o'clock saw the ladies preparing for bed, while Hampton and his uncle had one cigar, before retiring, in the verandah facing the river.

The cool night air blew refreshingly up its wide expanse. The fires of the native boatmen still flickered here and there, after their late evening meal. The tide rushed in broken eddies past embankment piles, or rippled musically against the bows of the numerous boats anchored in the stream, breaking up into tiny waves which caught the moon's rays and danced merrily away in long streams of light. The stillness was intense, broken at intervals by some (to Hampton) strange, unwonted sound. That blowing noise is the great river porpoise taking breath, as he rises slowly into air. Those harsh unearthly notes proceed from the conchs and gongs of one of the legions of temples adjoining. What hideous associations of human sacrifice and wild, mystic demon worship are conjured up by those barbarous strains.

Now it is the far distant cry, simulating human agony, of the coward jackal, answered at your very feet by some responsive member of the pack. Every dark nook and corner in the background of the moonlit scene is resplendent with brilliant fire-flies, gyrating in sparkling ever-moving columns, or spangled over the brushwood, mimicking in brightness the cloudless heavens above, which are powdered thick with twinkling gems. Solemnly, wonderfully beautiful is the night. This is the witching hour when the prowling tiger is out on his rounds, and Hampton almost expected to hear its deep gurgling roar break the painful stillness. Ah, what is that? Only the great vampire (the flying-fox) which falls with a startling crash plump into the midst of yonder mango tree, hanging if you could see it, head downwards, by the hooks in its wings.

Still they sit and watch till Hampton starts and, seizing his uncle (who is nearly asleep) by the arm, says, "See how those boats are rearing and plunging in the huge waves which have suddenly swept up the river, and look, it has torn that small one from its anchor!"

"It is only the Bore which comes up with the first of the flood," said Mr. Templemore, "you have seen a moderate one to-night, sometimes it is terrific, and accidents happen daily during the months of March, April, and May.

" To show the tremendous rapidity of its course, I may tell you that a few years ago, a small party of Europeans and natives gathered on the river bank at Howrah, opposite Calcutta, on the day of the full moon when the Bore is at its height, to watch its advent, at all seasons a most interesting sight. The whole of the native population who gain their living on the river are on the *qui vive*, and as they see the ebb languidly eddying down to the sea in its last struggle with the flood, they all push their boats into the mid-stream, and then patiently watch for their mysterious visitor. The tide comes to a stand-still, each man balances his oar or paddle ready to strike deep into the water to prevent his bark being turned broadside on, when hark, a distant hum is heard. It comes, Bân Bân (the native name for the Bore) shouts each excited boatman, and ere the words are well spoken the furthest line of boats is tossed as if in a tempest, and like a whirlwind it rushes up the river.

" Well, the party I mentioned were eagerly watching for the *dénouement* and stepped a few feet further out on a bastion or buttress than was prudent. The Bore was one of unusual violence, struck against the barrier presented by the buttress, and leaping over it, swept half of the spectators away."*

Let all these sights and sounds strike the fresh impressionable mind of youth and admit that an Indian night furnishes plentiful food for the imagination.

Hampton sat silently thinking, and began to realize how men of high chivalrous temperament might be fascinated by the wonders of that far off land. His reverie was broken by his uncle saying, "Seems strange to you Hampton, does it not? We must not sit too long in the night breeze, let us to bed, good night, my boy, good night."

Next morning at breakfast Mrs. Templemore asked her husband if he knew who Miss Browning could be. "Oh yes!" he said, "that must be a sister of Browning's on the staff. He has a very good appointment."

"I daresay we shall meet them at Mrs. Blandon's to-night," continued Mrs. Templemore. "By the by Laura, I hope you are clever at charades and those kind of things. There is generally great fun where we are going, and my friend deserves the highest credit for giving such pleasant entertainments. Were her example followed, Calcutta would not be noted as the most dismal place in India to pass an evening in. Heavy dinner parties and balls with their attendant late hours, are not suited to the climate at all. We shall go quite plainly dressed, and I hope to be home at something after eleven o'clock."

* The Bore or tidal wave comes up the Hooghly with lightning speed, and woe be to the boat caught by it in shoal water.

At eight o'clock that evening Mrs. Templemore's carriage drove under the portico of Mrs. Blandon's house in Chowrunghee.

We must now give a short account of the inmates of the house. First there was Mr. Blandon, a tall intellectual man, high up in the service, and very low down in debt, which forced him to remain in India. He was a model of good nature, and never interfered with his wife in her domestic arrangements. She was one of those evergreen women that even the hot weather of India cannot conquer, she was not pretty, but you could not be five minutes in her company without being fascinated by her. She brought you out if you could sing, and got you nice partners if you were a dancing man, sympathised deeply in your unfortunate rejection by that flirty Miss Jones, or winked at your sitting *rather* close to pretty Flora Smith in the verandah after that charming waltz. Then she had three daughters. Julia was grave, grecian and romantic. Florence was all smiles and curls and tricks. Edith, the youngest, sang splendidly and was rather plain, but that made her all the more gracious, and the numbers of little modest men, and stout middle aged bachelors, not to count blushing ensigns that she had made happy by volunteering to dance with them would fill a directory. No wonder with such aids Mrs. Blandon's house was so much frequented.

All three girls came down to receive Mrs. Templemore, and bore her and Laura in triumph up to the drawing

room, not forgetting to talk all the way up the noble
flight of stairs to Mr. Templemore, laughingly engaging him
to dance, and then glancing at Hampton in a way that sent
that gallant subaltern's heart into a palpitation at once. Mrs.
Blandon took Laura under her special protection, and made
her sit down beside her. In the mean time we must try to
describe some of the chief people in the room.

That lady with the black velvet and diamonds is the famous
Mrs. Kidnap. No one knows when she came out to India,
it is so long ago ; and that young man with the eye glass
and bushy hair, is her second husband. He went to propose
to one of her daughters, and the old lady liked his appearance
so much that she married him herself. In her day she has
been a very handsome woman. That little old man in the
corner is General Béhoos. He will not go to England, and it
is generally believed that, in private, he is a Hindu. That
stout important man with the sandy hair and whiskers is—
let me say it reverently !—Montmorency St. John Struggles.
He is a civilian, Commissioner of Khosamudpore ; has five
lacs in Company's paper ; is a widower and wants a wife ; he
has two ideas ; one that the St. John Struggles came down
from the planets (the truth being that his grandfather was a
ship chandler at Blackwall), and the other that India is a
vast hot bed, designed for the cultivation of good things for
his illustrious connections.

"Extension of the civil service," he is fond of saying, "is
what we want in order to govern the empire happily. There is

a great deal too much dragooning and soldiering and hectoring going on. Why, my sheristadar, Ramkinker mookerjee, and all my omlah say that since I took charge of Khosamudpore they are so struck with the high intellectual attributes of the white man, that they are half inclined to become Christians. Turn out your soldiers and interloping planters, and India would be a very different place."

Alack and alas, most potent Struggles, one short year and a storm will burst over your devoted head which will rudely dash your theories in your face.

The rest of the company consisted of young military men and civilians with a sprinkling of lawyers and merchants.

Amongst the guests Laura soon espied Mrs. Danvers and her daughter, and also Miss Browning, who seemed to have given up the idea of appropriating Captain Desmond to herself, and was listening most graciously to old General Béhoos, who, much to her apparent gratification, was giving her an account of *his* share in the first Burmese war.

It was not long before Captain Desmond came up looking radiant and happy at the prospect of spending the evening in our heroine's society. After begging her hand for the first dance, he whispered, " Do not think that I flatter Miss Templemore, but I must confess that your presence acts as a charm to drive away the demon of melancholy which follows me so perseveringly, and no wonder that such should be the case when you are so fairy-like, so enchanting." And in sober truth she was so. Her beautiful complexion softened

down by even the few days she had been in India, was shown
off by her simple dress of white muslin, and her arms and
neck looked so plump and white in their English freshness,
that even Montmorency Struggles could not suppress his admiration. "Splendid girl," he said to Mrs. Blandon, "Do
introduce me." "Mr. Struggles, Miss Templemore." "Ahem,
how do you like Calcutta." "Been to Government house
yet? Do you ride? Shall be happy to let you have one of
my Arabs." Here he was interrupted by the merry strains
of a waltz, and, much to his chagrin, Laura was claimed by
her partner.

The evening passed away merrily. When music was
wanted one of the sisters played. If a rest was required
one of them sang. A charade was got up in five minutes,
in which Hampton acted so charmingly that the sisters had
quite a little fight as to who should pet and praise him
most.

Laura had listened, during the intervals between the dances,
so attentively to Mr. Struggles' two ideas that, forthwith, a
flame of love sprang up in that great man's breast, uncon-
querable and consuming, and visions of Mrs. Struggles No. 2,
filled his mind. Fanny Danvers had her young civilian in
attendance, and Hampton wasted no more thought upon her.
He had already transferred his allegiance to the Misses
Blandon, but, as he afterwards confessed to Laura, they were
all so fascinating that he could not make up his mind which
sister he liked best. Laura laughed heartily at his dilemma,

and advised him to see how he could manage on his pay, before he attempted to think of a wife.

Mrs. Templemore was about to leave, and Laura had danced her last dance, when Captain Desmond came up and suggested that before going out into the air, she should walk a little in the broad verandah leading from the dancing room. He had been so devoted in his attentions, had behaved so differently to her from his general demeanour to women that she almost forgot her dislike to him.

" Miss Templemore," he said in a low voice, "Do say that if I try to deserve it you will treat me with less indifference than you have hitherto shewn. My regiment is ordered away up country, I shall only have a few days more of your society, but I shall go willingly if you will only say to me ' Hope.' "

Laura trembled at this, to her, unwonted language, and, had she been a flirt, would have led him on; but she resisted any little temptations to do so which might have been prompted by her woman's nature, and replied, " I am but a young and inexperienced girl, Captain Desmond, and hardly know how to answer you without giving you pain, but I must say it, I can give you no ——— "

" Hush," he said passionately, " Do not complete the sentence, I must, I will hope! Never have I felt for any one the entrancing feelings which your modesty and sweet ingenuousness have raised in my breast, and on the day I cease to hope, I shall be a broken-hearted man."

"Laura, you are very pale," said her aunt, as she returned to the room. "What is the matter?"

"I will tell you by and bye, dear aunt," she whispered, "spare me now or I shall betray myself."

Before Mrs. Templemore left, Mrs. Blandon mentioned that she had made up a pic-nic on Wednesday week, to be held at the Botanical Gardens. "I shall have a select party and hope to spend a pleasant day. We shall have lots of people to whom the place is new, and I hope the affair will come off with spirit."

Mrs. Templemore agreed to go, and after Julia and her sister had promised to be *such* friends with Laura, and had seen them all into the carriage, and said a hundred good byes, not forgetting a sly wave of the handkerchief to Hampton, they were whirled home, all charmed with their evening at Mrs. Blandon's.

"You see there was no fuss Laura," remarked her aunt, "no supper, and yet everyone was happy." When they were alone, the former recounted what had passed between Captain Desmond and herself, and said temperately but firmly, "I am afraid you will be much annoyed at what I have done, but I am determined rather to suffer anything than marry a man I do not love."

Seeing that Laura's attractions were likely to bring a host of admirers, and hiding her chagrin, her aunt replied, "I will not try to influence you, although I may think you very foolish to throw away such a good chance," and saying good night, hastily left her.

Laura lay long on her couch before she slept. The first open declaration of love had been made and she had spurned it from her. Had it been Conrad Daymer she thought, what happy dreams would have been conjured up before her. How strange that he should now represent her highest standard of merit. But, suppose he in return did not *really* love her. Doubts and fears, then hopeful dreams succeed one another as the hours pass by, and at last our heroine sleeps a troubled sleep.

The cold weather in Calcutta and all over India is a gay time. Every one makes up as much as possible for the imprisonment and disagreeables of the hot months, and from November to March there is a whirl of excitement; Government house balls, the Viceroy's private parties, and all the great officials receptions, take the first rank. Then come civil, military, and private balls, each vieing with the other in providing the finest music and most *recherché* suppers. Every thing is now so anglicised, that the new comer sees little in the arrangements differing from the customs at home. All old Indianism, as it is understood traditionally in England is done away with, sometimes to an inconvenient extent. To go to a dinner party even in May, in a complete black suit is "the thing," and as training will do a great deal, there are men in Calcutta, attenuated to that degree of condition, they do not seem to feel the heat. To see, however, some stout

Colonel from the north-west provinces, or a robust individual
fresh from home under the ordeal is painfully ridiculous.   A
ball is given in the hottest month (May) on the Queen's
birthday, and on that evening the quantity of red dye which
comes off the officers' coats on to the ladies' white dresses is
most laughable.   The uninitiated are rather alarmed when
they see the great red patches, but the habitués soon re-
assure them.   Flower shows at the Town Hall, fancy fairs,
and a round of visiting, fully occupied our heroine's time,
and she was delighted with everything around her.   She
was too sensible and thoughtful not to see, that such a life
might degenerate into a mere animal existence, but she was
young, everything was bright and new to her, so it was not
wonderful that she should have given herself up to a spirit
of enjoyment.

It had been by this time settled that Hampton should
go to Allahabad, he having been posted to a native regiment quartered there, and as he expected to be away a week
on his hunting expedition, he applied for his full privilege
leave of one month, and made all his arrangements to start
from Calcutta, immediately on his return from Kishnaghur.

One morning as Laura was reading the list of passengers
in the incoming steamer, she could not repress a little exclamation.

" What is the matter ?" said her aunt.

" Nothing particular," she replied, " only I see the name
of a friend amongst the passengers, who will be here on

Saturday." "A lady?" "No, a gentleman." "Young?"
"Yes." "And his name?" "Conrad Daymer. In my aunt's
last letter she said he had passed his examination for the
civil service, and would be in India soon."

Laura was glad to retire to her own room to think over
this new incident; would he call soon, and would he still be
interested in her? The thought that there might soon be
some one near her whom she might love, might look to for
protection, in that strange land, was almost too bright a
dream to be indulged in. True, her brother would do all
he could, but he was so young a soldier, duty or ambition might lead him to far distant lands, where a woman
would only be an incumbrance. She saw that her aunt's
affection was a mere show, and although she had faith in
her uncle, still he, good easy man, could hardly afford to
fight his wife for the sake of his niece. Poor thing she now
began to understand how girls may be sacrificed to men
that they do not love, and she wondered that the world
should so often condemn without a hearing the poor friend-
less creature who is goaded into a marriage of convenience.
This pity is all the more deserved by girls in India, where in
case of poverty there is not a single method by which they
may support themselves, and then comes that fatal item the
climate, which renders physical exertion in the plains impossible.

Marriage is the only escape offered, and many is the heart-
sick bride who has tried to smile amid her agony in that

gay city of palaces. Our remarks of course apply to those who are forced by circumstances to go to India, and who are left there destitute, or perhaps subject to domestic trials, which render any change acceptable.

As she was sitting pondering these matters in her own room, her aunt entered it and asked her if she would like to examine the interior of one of those immense piles of buildings she had noticed in the native town. "Templemore has procured me an invitation to go and see the widow of one of the richest Zemindars of Bengal. She is called the Ranee Rasmoney, her house is in Jaun Bazaar, and when we return home I shall tell you the history of the family."

CHAPTER V.

VISIT TO THE RANEE.   REVENUE SETTLEMENTS OF
BENGAL.

IN our last Mrs. Templemore and Laura were on the
point of starting to pay their visit to the Ranee Rasmoney.
The roomy double roofed palkee garee (closed carriage)
soon took them to the wide portals of her mansion in Jaun
Bazaar. This immense mass of masonry was built with a
large open quadrangle in the centre, and it was evident that
the architecture had, to a certain extent, been influenced
by the European buildings in other parts of the town. It
had therefore not so much grotesque ornamentation about
it as Hindu mansions generally have, and altogether wanted
the Moorish arches, minarets, or gorgeous mosaics so expressive of the taste of the Mahomedan conquerors of the
country. The windows which looked into the inner square
were barred with iron and seemed disproportionately small,
giving a prison-like look to the whole building. The roofs
of all four sides were flat, being formed of strong cement,
and afforded a spacious promenade for the almost imprisoned
inmates of the Zenanà. They were totally devoid of chim-

neys ; as fire-places, except in detached kitchens, are unknown in Calcutta, and were surrounded by heavy balus-
trades, on which might often be seen, pensively standing on
one leg, the great bone-eating adjutant bird. *En passant*
we may mention that three or four of these feathered giants
are almost always perched like sentinels on the lofty para-
pets of Government House, and having a revolting import
in their presence to the passer by, they are also to be seen
in expectant groups on the outer walls of that dreadful Gol-
gotha, the public burning Ghaut of Calcutta.

On stepping out of their carriage our fair friends entered
a lofty and rather gloomy archway, which pierced the
breadth of the building. Before them lay the quadrangle
which contained about an acre of ground. On each side of
the entrance were the guard-rooms of the door keepers
(Durwans) and armed retainers of the family. The walls
of these were covered with weapons strikingly similar to
those of the feudal times of England. Shining conspicuously out amongst them are lines of shields of the rhino-
ceros' hide, studded with silver bosses, each with its owner's
gaudy tulwar (scimetar) hanging underneath ; ranged
below, butt-ends on the ground, are fearful looking implements exactly like the Lochabar axe of the ancient Edin-
burgh guard, being a hook, an axe, and a spear in one.
Then there are iron-handled battle-axes, the counter part of
which the Black Prince may have wielded at Cressy or
Poictiers, mixed up with a host of other lethal weapons, in-

cluding the iron-bound lattee (bamboo) eight feet long and
heavy enough to fell an ox.

As the visitors entered the archway the motley turbaned
group of guards, their faces painted with caste-marks in
vermilion and white, stood up and salaamed.   They were all
picked men from the north-west of India, trained wrestlers,
and some of them gigantic in stature.   But—that fatal
" but"—a dozen Europeans would make the pantomimic
host fly, and as far as running goes, our gaudy friends
would certainly be unequalled.   The master of the cere-
monies, an elderly Brahmin, *his* face also caste-marked, and
with the nine times nine, twisted, sacred cord round his
shoulder, now receives our party.   He did not make the
usual obeisance, for no Brahmin, if he can safely avoid it,
salaams.   He puts his palms together before his face, says
" Asserbad" (blessing), and his salutation is over.   A sudra
or low caste man, in return, answers " Bundgee" (reverence), rubs the dust with his hand off the sole of the Brahmin's foot and puts it reverentially on his forehead.   Most
of the better class of natives in Calcutta speak English, but
the Ranee was a low caste woman, surrounded by bigoted
Hindus who affect contempt for the language of Christians,
and consequently it was not cultivated in her household.
Mrs. Templemore had, therefore, taken her Portuguese
Ayah with her as interpreter.   Led by the Brahmin, they
mounted a heavy flight of steps entirely of masonry, ending
in a solid iron-barred door and entered a corridor.   From

this they are taken into the state apartments meant to represent English drawing-rooms.   Here the bad taste of the
semi-savage shone out conspicuously.   Nothing but a London sale-room on an auction day, can afford a fit comparison
with these rubbish-filled halls.   Gaudy French clocks, outrageous French engravings, chandeliers of all sorts and sizes,
barrel-organs and musical boxes by the dozen, marble
tables, tawdry bead ornaments and common paper flowers,
here a shabby thing, there a costly one, make up what the
native does not really care for, but he hopes to overwhelm
you with his magnificence and says, "There, white man,
what think you of that."   Now they leave the show-rooms
and traverse another corridor, ending in a heavy purdah
(curtain).   A motherly-looking woman, neatly dressed, here
relieved the Brahmin, pulled the hangings aside, and they
entered a scantily furnished, matted ante-room.   A door
was then opened and they were in the presence of the far-
famed Ranee, who has a million in cash, and an income,
from land alone, of thirty thousand pounds a year.

Lalla Rookh, pearls, eyes of the gazelle, lights of the
hareem, fairy forms, and numerous other Orientalisms have
pervaded Laura's mind the whole of the morning, and the
reality is a little, fat, coffee-coloured woman, seated, to
please her guests, in a chair, with one muslin robe, the
Hindu sarree, round her body, and a handsome cashmere
shawl flung ungracefully over her shoulders.   She was
smoking and chewing pawn!   A dozen ill-favoured slave-

girls loitered about, two of them standing behind their
mistress's chair. The Ranee rose, shook hands, and begged
her visitors to be seated. The attendants then sprinkled
them with rose-water, contained in curious old gold bottles,
and put some otto of roses on their handkerchiefs. The
Ranee handed her pawn box to her visitors, who, however,
politely declined the contents of the same. Mrs. Templemore now made a frantic attempt to commence a conversation in her best Hindustanee, but bad was her best, and we
are sorry to say she broke down most woefully, making so
many horrible mistakes that she became quite alarmed, and
thankfully threw herself into the hands of her Ayah who
spoke for her.

" Was the Ranee well ? and how were the other members
of her family ? could she not see them ?"

" Oh, yes !" One of the slave girls was despatched with
a message, and in a few minutes in trooped something decidedly oriental at last. Still, being Hindu women, their
dresses were not so gorgeous as those of Mahomedan ladies
would have been. They did not wear the Turkish trowser
or the tight-fitting boddice, as these last would have done,
but some of their sarrees (the primitive Hindu dress in one
piece) were very splendid, being of cloth of gold, wound in
voluminous folds round their bodies, and brought over the
head mantilla fashion. One graceful girl particularly attracted Mrs. Templemore's and Laura's attention. We
shall try to describe her. She was about fifteen, and very

fair for a low caste woman. Her eyes were made to look doubly sparkling by the tint of soorma (black antimony) paste which had been painted on the edge of the lids. Her eyebrows joined, being slightly tattooed where nature had separated them. She had evidently a quantity of false hair, plaited in with her own, forming a very large knot (kopa) at the back of her head. In front her hair was parted in the middle, and she had actually two little croche cœurs on her temples. She was dressed in an airy tarlata-nish looking fabric (native made) of the darkest blue edged with gold, and covered with sprigs of the same. This was fastened round her waist, very full, drawn scarf-like over her body, and then lightly thrown over her head. She had on a magnificent pearl necklace and ear-rings. Her bracelets were solid bars of gold an inch broad, in which were embedded emeralds and rubies as big as beans. Her anklets were also very massive, and her slippers were one mass of gold embroidery and seed pearls. She seemed a favorite with the Ranee, and no doubt had been bedecked for the occasion. Of course she could neither read nor write, and being above the necessity of attending to the domestic economy of the household, what on earth she did to pass the time puzzled our heroine, and also seemed a poser to the Ranee herself, to whom the question was put by Mrs. Tem-plemore.

The other women were tall and short, ugly and pretty, stout and lean. They had all splendily jewelled nose-rings,

ear-rings, and some of them toe-rings. The only ornaments
Laura liked were the silver and gold solid huslees, or necklaces, made of such pure metal that they could be bent round
the neck by the wearer without any other fastening. She
also admired the gemmed bracelets and anklets, all of solid
gold, studded with uncut rubies and diamonds. One pretty
girl of about eight came up at her invitation, and she
was not a little surprised to hear that the little thing was
married, or at least betrothed. She had never seen her
husband, but that was nothing, and if he died she would be
a hopeless widow (as no re-marriage was permitted), would be
allowed no salt, where salt is a necessity, could wear no ornaments, and in fact would be glad when death released her from
her sufferings. Laura shuddered as Mrs. Templemore told
her this in a whisper. The women who had come in last were
the Ranee's daughters and granddaughters, for of course she
was a grandmother at thirty, with nephew's wives and her
own nieces all patriarchally living together—none of her
own sons lived past childhood, and in her old age she had
adopted a young man, who was such a character that we
must draw his picture separately. Before, however, doing so,
we must ask any learned reader where this old woman could
have procured a child with nearly auburn hair, lightish
hazel eyes, and a particularly stout though short frame.
His complexion was that of a dark Italian—not a bit
blacker—and not a soul in Calcutta knew how he could be
a native, and still be so fair. Besides, he was necessarily of

the same caste as his adopted mother, and that was a low one, which at once implies a dark colour. Certainly there are some queer things going on in native society, and the European is never a whit the wiser. If he had been a Mahomedan, of course a Cashmere woman or even an Eurasian, can easily be imagined as the mother; but here were rigid Hindus, to whom any outsider's touch is pollution, able to produce this strange fair boy. Verily, they are a clever race, and we suspect that Hinduism is a very convenient religion to the rich. This young gentleman had the finest four-in-hand drag, the fastest trotting English horse, and the best matched pair of Arabs in Calcutta. His barouche for the evening, and his harness, were radiant with silver and satin. He wore English pantaloons, a kimkhab, or gold brocade chupkun, or coat, and a little gaudy cap stuck on one side of a large bush of brown curly hair. He was the cynosure of all eyes, till one unlucky day, being probably intoxicated with his social success, he had the audacity, while driving on the course, to throw a rose into the lap of a very pretty little Englishwoman, recently married, and the wife of a Calcutta tradesman. Now came the contrast between white man and black, or at least semi-black. The irate husband, when he heard of the insult, procured a tremendous whip, laid in wait for his highness of Jaun Bazaar, drove his buggy alongside of the baboo's resplendent vehicle, and thrashed him well all up the course.

After a few minutes the ladies had exhausted their stock of questions, the younger native women had examined the (to them) extraordinary dress of the white women, and at last much to her horror, asked how many children Laura had ? Mrs. Templemore saw it was time to leave, for the old Ranee had tucked up one leg on the chair, and was making preparations to get up the other, which were evident signs of weariness, and so with smiles, and a good deal of dumb show supposed to be indicative of mutual affection, the party broke up. Several trays of sweetmeats, spices, and two handsome dacca muslin dresses were handed into the carriage, and our friends were glad to find themselves once more on the road to their comfortable home.

Mrs. Templemore now explained her reason for not giving the history of the Ranee's family. " The fact is," she said, "that I did not wish to disenchant you before our interview. The story goes that the Ranee's husband's father was Sirdar bearer (or head valet) to an old civilian nicknamed Jimmy Blazes, who wishing to pension the man off in a secure way, bought him—at a sale for arrears of rent—the Mokimpore zemindarry, or estate, for 8000 rupees, or £800. It was then certainly either uncultivated swamp or grass jungle, with but few inhabitants; still it was a great bargain. The family are of a low caste, and the title of Ranee or Princess, is granted by courtesy only, on account of their great wealth."

While the ladies are preparing for tiffin (lunch) we will

indulge in a few remarks on the subject of such estates as Mokimpore. It is the knowledge, come all too late, of such pretty bargains as the above which is the real cause of Sir Charles Wood, instructed by his council, putting so many obstructions in the way of the Bill for selling waste lands in India. The horse being stolen, the men who govern India double lock the stable. If we look over Bengal the amount of cases in which Government has been swindled is appalling.

The Rajah of Bettiah in the district of Chumparun collects a revenue of, it is said, two hundred and fifty thousand pounds per annum, having compounded with Government at the time of the perpetual settlement, for the sum of about twenty thousand pounds per annum, as his yearly rent. This is a grand instance. Here is a smaller one. A refugee Nepaulee got a grant of a tract of land in a remote corner of the district of Purneah, on a payment of thirty-five pounds annually. That tract comprises eight to ten thousand acres of rich land, and yields at least two thousand pounds a year. In a very small way, we have known a man pay six pounds to Government and collect three hundred and fifty.

To show that the native officials (in contra-distinction to the European) at the time of the settlement knew what they were doing, some few estates cannot now pay their government rents, their owners having neglected to bribe, and thus falling under the displeasure of the real pullers of the strings of the puppet Government. The bribe paid to the Bengallee Baboo, who really settled the Bettiah estate, the first on our list, was (it is openly talked of) fifteen thousand pounds down. What caused such terrible mis-management? it will be asked. The answer is the unparalleled ignorance of every one connected with government, of the districts under their charge, and of their languages and customs. To a certain extent this was unavoidable. Take a case. Suppose the civilian who settled the Bettiah estate, did go some eighty miles from head quarters with his tents to the spot (which we very much doubt, and which would be an impossibility for six months in the year on account of the heat), who was to tell him how far the Rajah's estate really extended to? There never had been any survey. His native staff were of course all bribed. If he rode ten miles of a morning one way, and in another direction in the evening to gather information, who was there to tell him anything. The villagers talked a nearly unintelligible patois, and were warned to say nothing that could injure the Rajah, on pain of ruin. The estate was some fifty miles long and the same broad, portions of it being notorious for deadly fevers. Any documents relating to it in the Government's hands were utterly worthless. Nothing but a detailed survey (by some one who understood the language &c.) could have given the extent of it, and then perjured testimony and forged documents would have been produced to show that perhaps a fourth of the real collection

was the proper rent charge. Under these circumstances
what was a man to do? Guess at it. He did, and the
results are known. Since the perpetual settlement of the
revenue, the country has galloped into prosperity, and in
looking at the matter it must be remembered that land and
everything else has risen in price in the most wonderful
way. Although Government has not one half the revenue
from Bengal that it ought to have, still the perpetual settlement has been the chief cause of the tremendous strides
that province has made towards material prosperity, and if
any one in England pictures its twenty millions of inhabitants as abject and miserable slaves, they are perfectly mistaken. In their own way they are happy, and in a few
more years their progress in wealth, civilisation, and perhaps Christianity will be something astonishing. There is no
doubt, also, that the perpetual settlement kept some parts
of Bengal quiet, during the late rebellion, and that the proper
way to prevent a recurrence of such a disaster is to extend
its blessings all over India. This one thing is the key stone
of our government, viz., let the native have his acre of land
at a lower rent than he knows his unprincipled and rapacious countryman would let him have it at, and he is yours
for ever.

In the first letters from the King of Delhi to the Zemindars of the north-west, the principal inducement offered for
them to rebel was " half-rents." The natives in the settled
districts knew the value of such a promise, and did not rise.

The hours seemed to pass slowly to Laura Templemore till the boom of the fort gun on Saturday announced the arrival of the Overland Steamer. She thought of her own anxieties, and wondered if Conrad Daymer had some kind friend to welcome him, and whether he would easily find out her uncle's house. Then there were letters to be received from her dear aunts, with all the news of Cheltenham and her old friends there.

To how many hearts, does the boom of that gun make the blood rush with quickened flow. To the merchant, its deep solemn voice, mayhap speaks of losses and redrafts and ruin, while to his neighbour, its sturdy bass notes, sing cheerily of profits and balances and success. To the parent, the husband, the lover, the brother, it cries, "come quick, come quick, we are waiting with beating hearts to fold you to our bosoms." The engaged one flies down to the steamer, perhaps to meet some fair charmer, he has not seen since childhood, but to whom he has plighted his troth by proxy. And verily this last is sometimes a most dangerous experiment. In proof of which assertion, list to the fate of Smith, assistant magistrate of Budsoorutnuggur. He was an outrageously ugly little man, all forehead and eyes like a frog or red mullet. He must have had two windpipes, for his voice, consisted of a shrill treble and a deep bass, which startled and astonished the listener by their jerky alternations. He must not only have been an ugly boy, but he had grown more and more ill-favoured yearly in India. No girl would look at him, although he was tremendously clever, and sure to rise in the service. At last a bright thought ; his cousin Lucy might; he wrote; she, desperate, said yes; transports of love; overland steamer; fascinating young officers; Lucy false; boom of the gun; brings her lover; squeaks from him ; almost shrieks from her ; fortnight given in Calcutta to consider the matter ; constant state of hysterics ; final answer—no ! Friend met him after a month. " Congratulate, Benedict," and all that sort of thing. (Smith lisped.) Hum ! She came outh, bat made thome widiculous excuthe abouth puthnal appeewance, and I am done again. Cost thwee hundred pounds out and home." Friend evaporated.

CHAPTER VI.

THE MEETING—TRIP TO KISHNAGHUR—BUFFALO
SHOOTING.

On Sunday Mrs. Templemore took Laura to the church
built by Daniel Wilson, late Bishop of Calcutta. We cannot say much for its architectural beauty, although it is a
handsome building on the whole. The internal arrangements were the most striking feature to our heroine.

The cold weather being nearly over, punkahs (large fans)
in continuous rows had been suspended from the ceiling at
a distance of seven feet from the ground, with a frill of one
foot deep depending from the framework, the result was
that most of the congregation were hidden from the clergyman, or, to say the best of it, only played bo-peep with him,
according to the punkahs' backward or forward motion. The
novelty was startling, but after a while the monotonous
undulation almost sent Laura and Hampton to sleep.

The rest of the Sabbath day was passed as it would have
been in England, but the contrast between a heathen and a
Christian land was conspicuously marked by the non-obser-
vance of the holy day by the great mass of the population,

who attended the Bazaars as usual, buying and selling. singing or abusing always in the highest keys, or squabbling over a disputed pennyworth of distressingly stale vegetables, or may be a slice of very high-flavoured fish.

Their knowledge, that is, of the uneducated, of the Englishman's religion is so very scanty, that they look on the Saheblog (ladies and gentlemen) going to church, as very much on a par with their own poojah worship at a shrine, and cannot realise why master and mistress should be more than usually solemn or meditative for one day out of the seven. Nor for the life of them can they make out why the house tailors are allowed a holiday by their mistresses on Sunday, the said knights of the needle improving the occasion by taking in piece-work at their own houses on that day. In the Moffussil (interior) where a church may be fifty or one hundred miles distant, poor isolated Europeans are apt to forget the return of the day of rest, and I have heard an ingenuous and reproving wife say to her thoughtless husband, why John *you must know* it is Sunday, don't you see the tailor has not come!!!

Monday morning brought the usual string of carriages and buggies to Mrs. Templemore's door, amongst whose occupants, the latest Calcutta gossip and the English steamer's arrival were the principal items of conversation.

" What do you think, Miss Templemore, of old General Béhoos, whom you met at Mrs. Blandon's, having proposed for Miss Browning? She has accepted him and the

marriage is to come off in a fortnight. There are even bets
he will have to be wheeled up to the altar in a chair, as the
excitement of the affair has brought on a tremendous attack
of gout in his feet. He has bought the bride elect some
magnificent jewellery, and the milliners have nearly gone
mad with the amount of orders they have received for laces
and silks."

Laura asked her informant if he were joking.

"Oh dear no," he replied, "marriages of this kind are
not uncommon here, old General Paugul was taken to the
church in a chair only last year, and *his* bride was only
seventeen, while Miss Browning, you know, is a *leetle* more
than that."

The day wore on—the visitors, one by one, left, and still
no Conrad came. Laura began to fear that she was forgotten, and felt almost sick with hope deferred.

And now 'tis only Mrs. Blandon's carriage, which is later
than usual, and *her* card which is brought in.

But who is this walking so demurely behind her, while
she smiles wickedly? It is he at last!

"I thought I should surprise you, Miss Templemore, but
Conrad is a cousin of mine, and as he seemed to consider it
life or death work to be here to-day, and asked me for your
correct address, I thought I could do no better than bring
him myself. Allow me to introduce him to you; Mr. Conrad Daymer—Miss Templemore." Here her eyes twinkled
merrily, and she could hardly suppress a smile.

One look and Laura saw rosy visions of the future rise softly before her.

The young friends did not speak a great deal, they were too much absorbed in thought to do so. They gazed with dazzled eyes down hope's sun-lit vista, and lost themselves in the enchanted scene. Everything round them aided the effects of love's intoxicating elixir, which they quaffed with eager lips. The perfume of the jasamine-scented chumpa flower mingled with the rose was borne into the luxurious, slightly darkened room, on the balmy, voluptuous air. The comparison with the ill-favoured natives outside, rendered Laura's beauty (and all beauty is comparative) the more striking to Conrad. Her dress was suited to the mildness of the climate, and was charmingly light and becoming. Youth's fair goddess lent all her grace to make our heroine beautiful. Truth and Innocence stood guardians by her side, and shed their light through her clear blue eyes; love tinged her cheek with softest tints and sparkled in her glance. Is it a wonder that Conrad felt entranced? Oh, glorious dreams of youth, clothed in bright rays from heaven, gilding our morning with their splendour and colouring even life's evening with chastened, but still beauteous hues, why last ye not for ever?

Alas, fair maid and brave youth, because this world would then be too much akin to Paradise, and ye would forget that dust must to dust once more.

Laura had never analysed her feelings to Conrad Daymer

when in Cheltenham. It was only after their separation
that she discovered how strong a hold he had of her imagination. Besides, her entry into the world's tumultuous
throng made her think of him as one who would protect her.
She felt that she could cling to him and defy all storms
which might burst around her; and when she saw by his
manner that she was all in all to him she was indeed
happy.

She and Conrad might have met for months, perhaps
years, in England, without their attachment ripening to its
full growth, but in India it was different. There genial
showers of rupees moisten the plant of love and beautify its
foliage and flowers, while youth's warm sun makes it grow
with a marvellous rapidity unknown in the cold north,
where want of means withers up the tender bud, or where
it is stunted by the freezing breath of counsel and warning
of the old, who, having plucked the fruit, grudge the next
generation even an experimental taste of its alluring clus-
ters. There are no old men so to speak in India, the pure
European population dies or returns to England before fifty,
and if one or two can be here or three pointed out who can
count their threescore years, notwithstanding the heat, hot
tiffins, and late whist parties, they are, we believe, merely
retained on special service as decoy ducks by the malevolent
spirit of the climate, whose insatiable appetite for victims is
never satisfied.

Monday evening being one of Mrs. Blandon's " at homes,"

Conrad looked forward with transport to the hour when he should meet her again, and talk over bygone days. They of course thought that neither Mrs. Templemore nor Mrs. Blandon had noticed any peculiarity in their meeting, but they were mistaken, and the former whispered to her friend in the course of her visit, " Laura will have her list full ere long, I think."

That evening was a happy one for the youthful pair, and the hours passed too quickly away; but they were to meet the next day, and perhaps the next and the next. The short periods of anticipated separation only giving a higher zest to the prospective pleasure of meeting, of interchanging thoughts, of comparing present experiences, all so novel, and past remembrances of far off old England, till I am afraid they were not very good company for the unsentimental portion of their fellow guests at the different houses at which they met.

Amongst other items of news circulated at Mrs. Blandon's *soirée*, was one which seemed to be of absorbing interest, it was that on the next morning a grand and very select hurdle race was to come off, which her aunt promised to take Laura to see. The riders were all to be young civilians. They were to be got up with extraordinary magnificence as to costume, and as some twenty of the prettiest girls in Calcutta were in hopes of catching the riders matrimonially, they would of course be present to see the affair come off.

Hampton was to start on his hunting trip after their return home, his party, therefore, left early, and we must, for a while, bid adieu to our Calcutta friends while we accompany him to Kishnaghur. Mr. Templemore's servants being old hands at dawk travelling, had packed Hampton's palkee with every necessary. Here a bottle of soda water, there a flask of brandy; a few oranges, a paper of biscuits and sandwiches, a loaded revolver, and the garrison was properly victualled for such a short trip, being only one of fifteen hours' duration. Think what it must have been to unprotected ladies who used sometimes to go a thousand miles by this conveyance.

The complement of men is eight bearers, one mussalchee or torch bearer and one or two bangyburdars, who carried conical boxes called petarahs slung on bamboos, containing the traveller's clothes. Every eight miles there is a relief, and, considering the weights carried, four miles an hour is not such a bad pace.

The extraordinary powers of endurance of the natives generally, and of the palkee bearers in particular, have astonished all Europeans who have witnessed their performance, and when the idea takes possession of some thoughtless, not to say inhuman, traveller that the natives 'can carry anything, the weights imposed on them are sometimes incredible.

Palkee travelling is the original native method of locomotion. These men are generally eight or nine stone in weight, their palkees are mere shells. Change this to a stout European weighing twelve or fifteen stone, add a tremendously heavy palkee, half a dozen bottles of fluid of some kind or other, a double barrelled gun, provisions, pillows, blankets, books, &c., and an aggregate is reached of at least 350 to 400 pounds. How four slight natives carry this at all is the wonder, but when they go for short distances at the rate of five miles an hour the feat becomes astonishing. We have known a thoughtless boy bring up in one of his boxes a bag of shot weighing twenty-eight pounds, and the men who carried it 300 miles had never even grumbled.

Hampton soon fell asleep, but, after being roused at the crossing of a small river or two, and being bumped on the ground at the relief stations, he found his night's rest would not be very satisfactory. The bearers have also a nice way of flashing the torch past the open door of the palkee, when they wish to ask for bukshish, which would enrage the mildest of human beings. It was about two o'clock next day when he reached the Kishnaghur Dawk Bungalow. Here he found a kind note, explaining the route, with a native Peon on a tatoo or pony who would act as guide.

" Four horses are laid for you" said the letter, "they are all good ones to go, so you ought to be here in time for dinner."

Hampton's first mount was a gay little government stud bred, which carried him like a bird, the road

was good, the native guide got up little races every now
and then to show off his riding, the weather was still cool,
and he was charmed with the prospect of sport before
him.

The thirty miles flew past therefore at railway speed, and
our hero found himself shaking hands with Mr. Besborough
in the noble verandah of Shikargurh house at about six
o'clock. He had been prepared by his uncle to see a fine
place, and to be hospitably received, but the reality far exceeded his expectations. There was an old English baronial
method of doing everything which astonished him. The floors
of all the lower rooms were of chequered marble, the roofs
were lofty, and the park of nearly a hundred acres studded
with splendid trees, was in capital keeping with the mansion.
A suite of rooms, a bearer, and Khidmutgar (table servant)
were placed at his disposal, and after a refreshing bath he
joined his host in the drawing-room. He there found as
warm a reception from Mrs. Besborough as from her
husband, and was introduced to some other ladies who had
accompanied their husbands to the hunting party, while
others were visitors from Calcutta.

"Our grand meet" Besborough told him, "was at
Christmas, and the present one is the last for this year.
We shall not have half as many sportsmen now, but I
have no doubt you will see some very dashing riding, and
some excellent sport."

Hampton did justice to his host's well-spread table, and

was delighted at the programme of the next day's hunting, which was discussed after the table-cloth was removed, and the ladies had left.

"What say you, Campbell," asked Besborough, of one of the most reckless horsemen in Bengal; "shall it be buffalo or pig to-morrow. I think myself that we had better try the buffaloes, before they think of shifting their quarters, for if we have one heavy shower of rain, they will be off south again."

The proposition was assented to, and Hampton was given a description of the nature of the sport, by one of the young fellows seated next to him. "There is a long line of marsh some distance from this," said he, "which extends about a hundred miles into the next province, Jessore. It dries up in the cold weather, and a herd of buffaloes, the last in this part of Bengal, sometimes comes up to our end of their feeding grounds. They are not likely to give us more than one day's work, as they think nothing of galloping fifty miles on end when they are thoroughly disturbed."

"If you are going out to-morrow," said his informant, " you had better stick to Campbell and watch what he does, he is the most renowned man amongst us at this kind of fun, and between you and me, it is no child's play." He explained that the buffaloes were ridden to, and shot at off horseback, with short carbines and pistols. "You have to go up quite close, for a bullet from a smooth bore does not do much more than penetrate the hide, if fired at any great distance. The ground is generally very bad, and if your horse slips while you are being charged, your chance of escape is small."

Hampton passed his first evening at Shikargurh very pleasantly, and was delighted at the cordial manner of the planters. He dreamt a good deal of buffaloes and wild boars, and other, to him, unknown monsters, and at last was enjoying a splendidly deep sleep when he felt the bearer's hand pressing his foot for the purpose of awakening him. He jumped up, and made out from his dumb show that the gentlemen were getting ready to start, although it was only five o'clock. He was soon dressed, and found his host sipping his coffee in one of the verandahs, where a table was laid with a light breakfast.

"Good morning," he said, "slept well I hope after your ride. By the bye, what kind of horseman are you? I ask you this because riding buffaloes is ticklish work, and our animal is as superior to the American bison, as a wild boar is to a tame one. Our buffalo bulls never run except to keep up with the herd of females, and always take the post of danger. They stand sometimes sixteen hands high at the shoulder, and are magnificent creatures. The tiger dares not go near them, and very few elephants will stand their charge. When separated from the herd by rivalry, they are called 'Urna' by the natives, and are terribly mischievous. We shall stalk up to them to-morrow behind a couple of native carts loaded with straw, with our horses following, and when we come pretty near we must gallop right at them and disable as many as we can. I think you had better remain close to Campbell here, as in case of a mistake, he is *the* man to help you. I have ordered my steadiest Arab, and you will find a pair of pistols in the holsters of his saddle. You shall also have a nice light carbine, which I have lately had out from England. I am going to send out some elephants, as we may hear of an urna bull after we are done with the herd."

The party started, and rode gently up to the edge of the low lands where the buffalo ground commenced.

At one time the whole vast expanse of country had been a sheet of reed and grass jungle diversified by patches of water, but villages were beginning to be formed on the skirts of what was destined to be valuable rice ground, and the grass jungle was not now so continuous. In the rains the whole country was a sea, and might be sailed over for hundreds of miles; a strange thing it is to be going along all sail set, in one of the beautiful boats used by the Jessore planters, over miles and miles of the thick rice crop peculiar to the district which grows sometimes in as much as ten feet of water. The boat will be gliding along seven or eight miles an hour. In the direct tract appears that which to the new comer seems a field of beautiful grass waving two feet above the water. He expects a terrible shock, but no! the boat slides in among the thick vegetation and will be brought up all standing by it, if the breeze should

fail at all. In some places of these wild jheels of Bengal,
the surface of the clear water is covered for acres with the
beautiful white or rather pink lotus of the Hindu mythology.
The broad dark green leaf completely covering the surface
of the water, contrasts beautifully with the gorgeous flower,
which sends up a faint perfume as you draw up your boat
to gaze your fill on the wondrous sight. How paltry does
the display in some famous hothouse appear to those who
have seen such a sight as we attempt to describe! There
one flower is watched with tender anxiety, here you may
load your boat if you like, without making any gap in the
glowing parterre. Talk of loading your boat. No sooner
said than done. The boatmen make a delicious vegetable
curry from the peeled stalks, and soon have a hundred-
weight stowed away for future feasts. As they tear the
long plants from the bottom, look over into the clear depths,
and wonder at the swarms of fish darting about. At the
time of the rice ripening, great sport is afforded in these
jheels by the flocks of wild geese and ducks, which migrate
from the shores of Siberia, and spend their winter in the
tropics. No words can convey an idea of their incredible
numbers or diversity of species.

We must now return to our subject. The buffalo of this
part of India is almost amphibious, swimming about for
hours, and diving when necessary for his food, which is sub-
merged by the rise of the rivers in the rainy season. At
night they retire to some comparatively high ridge, where,

the bulls acting as sentinels, they sleep securely. Their strength and courage is very great, and they roam about the terror of the squatter who may have cast his lot in these lately cultivated wilds. Even the great man-eating (in contra-distinction to the fish-eating species) alligator generally avoids the neighbourhood of the surging mass of shining black horns (six and seven feet long) of a herd of buffaloes; but once within the writer's experience, one of these monsters, having been tempted by a nice fat calf, forgot his usual caution and seized the tempting morsel. A cry of pain, answered by the mother, and caught up by the herd, brought them down in a mad plunging gallop to the spot, which was covered with three feet of water, and adjoined a broad river. The result was that the alligator was gored, trampled on, tossed from horn to horn, and made mincemeat of in five minutes. The sight was magnificent. Fancy the spray thrown up by a thousand hoofs, while the air resounded with the deep grunting roar peculiar to the animal, and the clash of the horns as they threw their victim about.

Hampton's heart beat quick when Campbell, lightly touching his shoulder, whispered to him to peep from behind the straw which hid them from the buffaloes. There they were some five hundred yards off, all facing the danger which they began to suspect. One or two magnificent bulls stalked slowly to the front, their horns thrown back, and their noses in the air. A series of deep grunting signals passed through the herd, and the old sportsmen knew that it was time to be up and doing. A rush was made for the horses. The movement was at once seen, and with a sound of clashing horns and thundering hoofs, the unwieldy monsters bounded across the plain, followed by the eager hunters. On bad, soft ground, a horse has no chance in speed with a buffalo, but it is not so on good. The horsemen were therefore soon up with them, and shots were fired on all sides. Some of the cows, heavy with calf, or with little ones by their side, soon separated from the rest, and were easily overpowered by the less adventurous spirits amongst the riders. But Besborough, Campbell, and one or two more singled out the bulls, and rode quickly and steadily till they could get along side. As we have said before, the male buffaloes are perfectly fearless. Their object, therefore, in keeping behind was to save the cows and calves who are now beginning to be blown by the tremendous pace, and, on their approaching some heavy grass cover dived here and there into it in small parties. When we talk of grass our readers must remember that it grows to a height of eight and ten feet in Bengal.

Hampton had kept up steadily on Campbell's left hand, watching all his motions and wondering when *their* part of the play was to begin. Neither of them had as yet fired a shot. The latter now pointed to an enormous bull, which, bewildered at the separation of the cows, was galloping along after a few of them which still kept together.

"Now, Templemore," said he, "take a pull on your horse, and we'll make a dash at that big brute, but reserve *your* shots, for if we don't hit him hard, I am afraid from the look of the ground (which was becoming wet) that we shall not have time to reload. You had better let me fire first, and then you can go in and see what you can do."

Neither of the plucky Arabs wanted spurs, a jerk of the elbow sent them at racing pace up to the bulky monster, who, with the white foam gathered round his mouth, glared back on his pursuers with his vicious black eyes, and was indeed a formidable foe. Keeping about twenty paces on one side of him, Campbell fired one barrel of his carbine right into his shoulder, but it did not stagger him at all; he only seemed to put on more steam, and went faster than ever. The ground, as Campbell had foreseen, became a little heavy, and the horses did not go quite so freely. He feared that they would lose their prey if he was not brought up at once, so he daringly rode up close to his shoulder. He fired. His horse slipped. The buffalo saw his chance, and before he could recover himself, rushed on him. He gave a side sweep of his horns, which would have thrown horse and rider on the ground like nine-pins had he touched them, but he luckily almost missed his mark. One horn went through Campbell's jacket, underneath his braces and would have lifted him from his saddle had these not snapped in two.* The active little horse

* This is a fact.

did his best to get out of his enemy's reach, and bounded forward.

Hampton, who had anxiously been watching the fray, now dashed his horse up and fired both barrels right into the buffalo's face. This staggered him, but not being injured mortally, he only stopped short, deliberated for a moment, then turned and swung once more into his long clumsy gallop. The tournament was over. In the melée Campbell's carbine had been thrown into the mud and trampled on, smashing the stock. His horse was going slightly lame, and the bull was every moment increasing his distance from his pursuers. The ground was getting worse and worse, so for once the hitherto unconquered sportsman had to give in.

" It would be madness for you, Templemore, to go after that ironsided brute by yourself, so you must be content with what you have done. That was a narrow squeak I had," he said to his companion as they rode slowly back, "I am much indebted to you for taking off the animal's attention when you did, or he probably would have had me again before my horse had thoroughly recovered himself."

Hampton expressed his pleasure at having been of service, but was much disappointed at not being able to say that they had been successful in their pursuit.

On reaching the main party, they found that two or three cows had been knocked over, and a fine bull was just on the point of giving in to the numerous wounds he had received.   One of his front legs was broken at the knee, and it was piteous to see the noble animal, when he tried to charge his destroyers, come down headlong, as his shattered leg gave way under him.

"Bring up the big rifle," said Besborough, "and I will put him out of his pain."

It was taken out of the bowdah of the elephant belonging to that gentleman, which had come up to the scene of action, and, walking to within a few paces, he sent an ounce ball into the beast's head.   This ended his struggles and he sunk with a low groan on the grass.

Campbell recounted his adventure, and Hampton was not a little complimented on the part he had taken in the matter.

CHAPTER VII.

COMBAT BETWEEN AN ELEPHANT AND BUFFALO.—
ENCOUNTER WITH A TIGER.

IN our last, Campbell and Hampton had just rejoined the main party of sportsmen. "I sent him with you, Campbell," said Besborough, laughing, "to be looked after; but the tables were turned—he looked after you. Now," continued he, "it is useless thinking any more of that herd, they are miles off by this time. What say you to try for the Urna bull which my mahout says the villagers have reported to him as living amongst the crops, defying every one, and destroying everything that is sown?"

Campbell and the rest of the party were delighted to prolong the day's sport, so, changing their horses for elephants, and light carbines for rifles, they steered for the village in which the solitary bull had taken up his quarters. They were not long in learning something about him. "He tossed Sheyk Ruheem's mother clean over the hedge of her yam garden yesterday, curses be on him to the seventh generation," said an old man they met. He forgot to say that the aged dame had thrown an earthen pot at the buffalo, and abused him, as only Bengalee women can abuse, for trespassing on her domain.

"He ate up half my new-planted sugar cane the other day," added another. "Oh, he is a brute, and his eyes are like balls of fire." Warming in his description, he made out that the buffalo was about ten feet high, and would scatter the elephants like chaff.

"We'll see about that," said Besborough. "You give us some one to show his whereabouts, and we will stop his sugar cane eating for the future." The man sent one of his sons, who, crossing the village, led them to a highly cultivated plain. On reaching the middle, he pointed with his hand, and said, "He was last seen in that ruhur field, and may be there now; so, please your lordships, I'm off to that mango tree, and you can find him out for yourselves."

The ruhur stands about six or eight feet high, and yields a kind of pea, used all over India to make dall with. This, we may explain, is nothing more than split peas which are boiled nearly into a soup, and eaten with rice.

The elephants were formed into line, and beat slowly down the field, crushing and eating the crop as they went along. Suddenly they left off feeding, and the low trumpetings and beating of trunks on the ground show that there is something ahead.

"There he is!" shouts a sportsman in the middle of the line, and Hampton saw a splendid pair of horns glance over the high cover. No sooner did the buffalo see his enemies than, with a loud grunt, he charged right down on them. Crack went every rifle, but, going at the pace he was, and being hidden in the bushes, he was only hit slightly in one or two places. The wounds infuriated him the more, and he made steadily for one of the elephants, who, coward like, turned round and received the charge behind. The shock was terrific, and nearly sent him on his head. He recovered, but the buffalo charged home again, and this time stuck one horn into his hip. He roared with agony, and ran into the open with the animal still goring him. Besborough was riding the famous male elephant called Hadji Baba, valued at five hundred pounds, and renowned all over Bengal.* He was taken up as quickly as possible, and his rider put two balls into the bull, which made him turn with fury on him. Now came a sight worthy of an imperial arena, and which has not often (if ever) been witnessed by any of the present generation of sportsmen in India.

With the blood streaming from his wounds, he made a desperate rush, and was received on Hadji Baba's massive tusks. Unluckily, these last, according to custom, had been deprived of their tips, and were bound round with handsome silver bands, partly for ornament and partly to prevent the ivory splitting. The blunt ends, therefore, could not pierce his tough hide, but only served to press him back, making his ribs crack again, for, powerful as the

* The Hadji originally belonged to Col. Gairdner, 16th N. I. He died, eventually, of fever brought on by a single combat with a tiger.

monarch of the swamp was, he had his master now before
him.   He dashed his horns right and left, trying to get
under the elephant's guard, but his efforts were useless.
They push, they strain, the ground is torn up by their
desperate struggles.   At last Hadji Baba knelt down, and
inch by inch forced his opponent back, till, with one good
heave, he sent him on his side.   The spectators of this
tremendous fight had not been able to get their elephants
up near enough to enable them to fire with certainty; their
animals, notwithstanding mighty sounding blows from the
heavy driving irons used by the mahouts, having bolted in
all directions the moment the fight commenced.   One or
two of the staunchest, however, were at last urged up, and
as the buffalo fell over, two or three balls were put into
him.   He rose, staggered a few paces, stopped, swayed to
and fro, and then fell to the ground.

Besborough had not, of course, been able to fire after the
fight commenced, and had held on to his howdah for bare
life.   He was enchanted at the way his mahout, as well as
his old favorite the Hadji, had behaved, and at once
promised the former a handsome bukshish.

Every one now dismounted to view their prostrate foe,
and an animated discussion took place as to who was to
have the horns, hoofs, &c.   After a great deal of laughing,
joking, and brandy-and-water, it was decided that Hampton
was to have the former to take to his uncle, and to give
greater *éclât* to the occasion, an old Scotch assistant of

Besborough's, who, I am sorry to say, was much too fond of whiskey (and, in fact, was a privileged pensioner of that gentleman's), insisted on mounting the back of the dead animal, glass in hand, and giving them a slight oration. "Ye see, gentlemen, that it wad be a maist inveedious thing to gie the spoils o' this muckle black deevil to any other than oor young military friend, wha has distinguished himself in a way that wad no hae disgraced Wallace or Bruce, or any ither of our immortal Scottish heroes. I therefore propose that we mak the horns a present to him, to be safely delivered in Calcutta, and mairover I beg you to drink Mr. Hampton Templemore's health with three times three." Amid shouts of laughter old Macsneeshan continued, "Hip, hip, hurrah!" when lo and behold the buffalo slowly rose, and walked away with the petrified Scot astride on his back.* "Haud him, shoot him, or I'm a dead man," screamed Mac, and a dozen rifles were raised to knock the bull over again, but it was soon seen that such means were not necessary to secure him. It was his last struggle. As Macsneeshan fell off on one side, he dropped down so suddenly that he nearly shook his horns out of their sockets.

"Well, Mac, how do you feel?" said Besborough, addressing his friend, as he sat the picture of astonishment on the ground. "Hech, sir, I'm clean dazed; and if ye hae a drap o' Glenlivet in your flask, just hae the kindness to hand it to my mouth, for my ain hands tremble sae I hae

* This is a fact.

my doubts whether I could help mysel, and it wad be an
awfu' peety to waste good liquor by spilling it." Besborough did as he was requested, and, amid a chorus of
laughter, the old Scotchman was helped into his howdah.
Hadji Baba was not hurt in the conflict, but he was fright-
fully excited, and was taken home at once under charge of
two female elephants, who coaxed him along, and it was a
week before he would eat willingly, and, although a splendidly tempered animal, he tore down everything that came
in his reach when taken out, for some time.

It was voted unanimously that the party had had enough
for one day, so the cavalcade wended their way home, short-
ening the road by smoking, talking, and laying plans for
the morrow.

Hampton could hardly believe that he had been one of the
actors in such stirring scenes, and promised himself not a little
satisfaction when he should recount his doughty deeds to
Laura, or send home an account of them to Jack Sterndell.

He thought he had never seen such a glorious set of
fellows as the Kishnaghur planters, and he was right, for
at the time of our story the district could boast of as fine
a set of men as ever earned the name of sportsmen. They
were splendid in the field, and hospitable after a fashion
not known elsewhere, for they had not only the kindly spirit of
the settler in new countries, but they were wealthy, and could
offer their guests every luxury that money could command.

Hampton had already had half a dozen invitations to go

and "spend a month with me, old fellow," but he was obliged to disappoint all his would-be hosts by saying he must join his regiment in a week or two.

If he thought highly of the guests at Shikargurh, great also was his contentment at the breakfasts and dinners spread before him. Hardly any luxury to be had in England was wanting, while the numerous native dishes, and the turbaned line of servants (each guest bringing his own) gave a most imposing look to every meal. Here he tasted, at breakfast, the real "Nawabee Pillaw"—rice, butter, almonds, raisins, and spices, piled up in fascinating confusion over a tender joint of lamb or pair of well-fed chickens. Cutlets, done to a turn, of the splendid Biktee and Ruhoo fish, invoked him by their crispy brownness to eat them. For the first time in his life did he find wild ducks so common that a savoury stew was made of their breasts only, sliced fine in a gravy the secret of which the old Khansamah (butler) would not divulge for untold gold. Here the plump quail and still plumper little ortolan afforded gentle amusement after the graver labours of the table, while the piquant Bombay duck (a kind of dried fish) gave zest to the vintages of Lafitte or La Rose. Oh, those glorious feasts at Shikargurh. Youth, health, hunting —a kind welcome, and a hearty good wish at parting—what more was wanting to make them perfect?

Mr. Besborough, Hampton's host, was proprietor of the largest indigo estate in Lower Bengal. It extended over some four hundred square miles, had thirty or forty factories for manufacturing the dye, with about thirty thousand acres of land (held in lease from the natives) actually cultivated in indigo, while the remainder grew crops such as rice, sugar cane, linseed, &c. The business was superintended by Mr. Besborough and a dozen European sub-managers and assistants, who had again under them a staff of natives of all ranks and castes, numbering, perhaps, one thousand. In a good season the concern produced about £80,000 worth of the dye, on an expenditure of about £50,000. All this development of the resources of the country resulted from the energy of a small body of Englishmen, but for whom the whole tract of land would have been in the same savage state in which it was found some fifty years ago. Then there were no roads, no money; oppression for the poor, immunity from punishment for the rich, were the order of the day. The good change came by the advent of the much-maligned indigo-planter, who rented lands from the native proprietors at such remunerative rates that, whereas their fathers and grandfathers had generally been content to live in mud-built huts, the present race of zemindars rejoice in grand brick-built mansions, painted and bedecked as Hindoos love them to be. They have also now accumulated sufficient wealth to become indifferent to the white man's gold, and to hate the influence which he, from his vastly superior energy and honesty, commands from the masses of the people. This feeling, a rise in the price of all native products and in the rent of land and labour, all combined to cause the indigo riots which took place some few years ago in Lower Bengal, and which, backed by the countenance of the Government officials, some of whom shared in the jealous feelings of the zemindars, ruined a most meritorious body of men, many of whom had been toiling for thirty years. We believe that a reaction has now taken place; and when we see the very men who hated such things while in Bengal, becoming the directors of joint-stockeries in London, whose result will be the introduction of more and more Europeans into India, it is probable that the unfortunate Bengal planters may yet recover some of their ancient prosperity.

As Mr. Besborough had some work to do in his cutchery, or office, Hampton volunteered to accompany him, and was not a little astonished at the mob of clerks or native writers, accountants, rent-collectors, land-superintendents, &c., &c., who swarmed out of the verandahs and different rooms at the approach of the burra sahib (great gentleman). This being a holiday, Mr. Besborough did not go through his usual routine of work, which consisted of auditing accounts, hearing Bengalee correspondence, settling disputes between tenants, and many such matters. He contented himself with an hour or so of business. Here is a sample of the cases brought before him. There has been an up-and-down fight between the grain-seller and hide-skinner of the nearest village. " Protection, most noble lord!" shouts the former, holding out a bunch of hair which had been torn from his top-knot.

" Justice!" moans the latter, with outstretched arms; "see how my life has been taken; look at these wounds!"

These, to say the truth, are not very frightful, being scratches made the most of by assiduous rubbing.

" What is the case?" inquires Mr. Besborough.

" My cow!" responds the grain-seller.

" My wounds!" groans the hide-skinner.

And so they would go on with their frenzied duet were they not forcibly made to sit down while the quarrel is explained by a bystander.

The grain-seller's cow died suddenly last night, and he swears that the hide-skinner poisoned it, to get the hide. But how is this to be proved? No one would cut up a cow in Bengal for love or money—the Hindoos from religious scruples, and the Mussulmans from fear of the Hindoos. Analysis of the cow's stomach, therefore, was impossible, even if she had not been eaten up entirely by the jackals and vultures an hour or two after her death. All the native servants are against the poor hide-skinner, who is of the lowest caste, it being pollution to be touched by him. For this very reason Mr. Besborough sides with him as long as possible, but nothing can be made of the affair from the contradictory evidence adduced, so, with an intensely judicial look, he said, " You are both sons of the evil one, to fight in this way. The order is that you be fined one shilling each, and sign an agreement to keep the peace." This was a trifling case, but in purely native society the skinner might have been half killed and expelled from his home, there being no justice for a low-caste man. Suitors and servants were on the point of being dismissed, when an old Brahmin came up and made his obeisance, which was politely acknowledged.

"What are your wants to-day, Bisnanth Acharjea?" "Cherisher of the poor! I require the services of your house-watchman." "In what way?" said Mr. Besborough. " Incarnation of religion! your watchman is the head thief of the country; and if you will only give him a hint, my bullock, which was stolen last night, will be quickly restored." Mr. Besborough seemed to believe that this was not far from true, and sent for the aforesaid watchman, by name Dursun Gwala. "Dursun, do you hear what the Brahmin has been saying?" "Yes, my lord." "Well, that bullock must be returned, *sharp*." "How can I return it?" whines the arch-thief; "I have no power."

"Yes, you have," rejoins Mr. Besborough, "and the bullock *must* come back." "Good, my lord," mutters Dursun; "if any of my boys have it, it will be found tied up near the Brahmin's house to-morrow after dusk." "Did you ever hear of such a scoundrel?" asked his host, turning to Hampton. "I and all other Europeans are obliged to keep the sirdars, or chiefs of the gang of thieves, as servants. Did we not do so, our cattle and goods would not be safe for an instant. That fellow Dursun does not thieve himself, but he knows of every robbery in this part of the country. I have known him trace a bullock for forty miles, from village to village, and bring it back to its owner, charging, of course, handsomely for his trouble." The Brahmin folded his hands, salaamed, and retired, while our friends wended their way back to the house.

On Hampton's second day it was decided that they should beat some very heavy cover in an old deserted village, part of which had been swept into the Ganges, forcing the inhabitants to retire a mile or two inland.

Their host did not accompany them, and the leadership of the party was entrusted to Campbell. As the morning fog cleared away, the hunters found themselves at the edge of the jungle.

"Take care of your head to-day," said one of the old hands to Hampton; "about the most dangerous things in village hunting are the over-hanging branches of trees, which will knock you out of your howdah if you don't look out. Again, never urge your elephant too fast; if you do so, the driver and he may get flustered, a bolt under the trees will ensue, and you are done for."

The order was given, and they advanced. It was a wondrous sight, that tangled mass of vegetation : who shall describe it ? Now the treacherous hooked streamers of the rattan seize on howdah trappings, your hat, your coat. If you advance, they will be torn to pieces. Carefully

each hook is undone, and you slowly creep along. The
ground, where it can be seen, is a crumbling black mould,
rich with the decayed leaves of centuries. There is a damp,
fetid, feverish smell about the place. Now a group of Areca
(betel-nut) palms, graceful as the trees of fairyland, shoot
up to the light. They are fifty feet high, straight as an
arrow, without a branch, and no thicker than one's arm.
In the open, one blast of wind and they would be down;
here they are supported by their closeness to each other
and by their stalwart neighbours, the mango and the
tamarind.

Numerous, to him unknown, animals attracted our hero's
eye as they plunge deeper and deeper into the forest. The
beautifully marked Khutass, or civet cat, of Lower Bengal,
runs with wondrous activity along the branches of that
splendid evergreen, the Jack tree (*Arto carpus incisa*), and
is out of sight in a moment. Lazy jackals, retired for the
day, wonder why their dark haunts are invaded in such a
rude manner. The pretty little gray-and-white squirrel
seems almost paralysed with astonishment, and allows
Hampton to nearly put his hand on his tail. The great
tree lizard glares at him with his protruding eyes, and gets
out of the way most unwillingly, having nearly induced a
silly fly, for which he has been watching, to come and be
eaten. Insects in myriads harbour in every trunk and
bough and leaf. The wild silkworm builds his cocoon in
yonder Peepul. Here, on your arm, settles the wonderful

green butterfly, not to be distinguished from the leaf of a
tree. Whew! now you have a colony of the big red ant
scattered over you. Brush them off carefully and quickly,
for if you have bad blood and they should sting you, they
will make your arm swell into a bolster in a few minutes.

As the elephant slowly passes the fork of that huge
Tamarind, see clustered together a heap of beautiful rose-
coloured beetles, spotted with black, two inches long, and
most charming to the eye. On that tall tree, withered by
the lightning's stroke, are hanging in dozens (by the hooks
in their wings), head downwards, the huge bat (the fruit-
eating flying fox) as it is called, and on its neighbour, that
gigantic cotton tree's topmost branches, is gathered together a huge bunch of dried brushwood, which is the bald-
headed vulture's home, her hideous brood being now and
then visible as they crane over to look for their dear parents,
who are, perhaps, enjoying themselves at some ghoul's
feast miles and miles away, or soaring on broad-stretched
pinion in wide-sweeping circles, a mere speck in the vault
of heaven, from which their wondrous eyesight will enable
them to mark the fall of patient ox, or body of wretched
Hindoo floating down great Gunga's tide.

But we must cut short our catalogue or it would become a book in itself and attend to our sport.

The line of elephants moves slowly along, here pulling
down a juicy branch, crushing it between their millstones
of teeth, or wantonly planting their ponderous feet against

the tall saplings which stop the way, and bending them to the ground. At last they all met in an open space.

" I hear," said their leader, " that there is a tiger, tigress, and two cubs in this jungle, but it will be a tough job to get them out. We can at any rate beat the remaining half of the forest, and then, if nothing starts, we will try back."

" Advance !" is again the word. In a few minutes the elephants show by their uneasiness that their ancient enemy is not far off. By this time the party had approached the bank of the river, which was on their left. Campbell, Hampton, and two others, formed the line on that side, and were all within speaking distance of one another. Suddenly Hampton's mahout seemed galvanized, and without speaking, pointed with his hand, and there, sure enough, gliding quietly but quickly away, was a noble male tiger. He was sleek and glossy, being well fed on the village cattle which fell into his hands—or rather claws. The feeling which is generally experienced on first seeing the jungle monarch was also shared by Hampton. He wondered and admired, and almost forgot that he had to fire. A moment or two sufficed to collect himself, and the ring of his rifle echoed through the wood, but he has missed. Now Campbell sees him, and he also fires, but the ball only buries itself in a tree. The tiger has a charmed life, and is lucky in having such heavy cover to hide himself in. He is driven out of two or three heavy patches, and at last seems inclined to make for the river. Tigers swim like otters, and if once he takes to the water he will make for one of the islands and be lost.

The hunter nearest him, shouted to Campbell, "he is going to swim for it, what shall we do?" The elephants could not be taken fast enough through the cover, to stop this manœuvre, at least not fast enough to please the impetuous Campbell, he therefore, who ought to have known better, made his animal kneel, jumped off his back, and rifle in hand rushed in pursuit.

"Follow me," he cried to those nearest him, and in a moment Hampton and two others joined him. They clear the trees. In front lies a hundred yards of sward smooth as a bowling green. He is down the bank, no doubt, and the first up, will get the best shot. All four race to the spot.

What stops them in their breathless haste? What means that broken exclamation of horror? What, that slight inch by inch recoil from some dread object in front? The men are close together in a little line. They glare at something before them.

There! just sunk under the bank, watching them with his cold relentless eye is the tiger! He is motionless, but for a convulsive twitching of his limbs. His lips are drawn up over his shining fangs, in a horrid grin, the bristles of his neck are stiff and erect.

Now gallant Englishman show your pluck! now prove that shoulder to shoulder, nothing mortal can make you

9

flinch! Now Hampton think of your gallant father, and bear yourself as his son ought to do!

Campbell was the bravest of the brave, and he knew the result of the slightest symptoms of hesitation. Placing himself firmly with one foot slightly advanced, he hoarsely whispered, "Stand like men, don't waste your shot for God's sake," when the tiger, with a gurgling roar, was on them. Bang! bang!! He rears in the air, tears at the bullet wounds with his teeth, falls, but again writhes forward in mortal agony. Bang! bang!! four barrels more. The blood and foam bubble from his mouth, a few furious struggles, and he is dead!!!

No cheers, no hurrah, silently the four men grasp each others' hands, and draw a deep long breath. The bullet marks are all there. Hampton, young as he was, was true as steel, and his ball had gone straight as the rest. Campbell put his hand on his shoulder and walked slowly back to their elephants. "I was very wrong to lead you into such a trap," he said, "and should never have forgiven myself if anything had happened to you, but it's over now, and you have had a trial which never fell to my lot before."

The men on the right of the line on hearing the firing, had made to the river side also, but only in time to see the tiger fall.

"That fellow Campbell will be killed some day," said one of them; but he was wrong, for after a few years' sojourn in India, he returned to England still in the prime of manhood, and is alive now to talk over his exploits in the far East. The remainder of the village was beaten, but the tigress and her cubs were not at home, and sooth to say the events of the morning had cast a shade of gloom over the party, and rendered them careless about the matter.

"What say you to knock over some hares and partridges?" said one of the party.

This was agreed to, and they shot their way home on foot, making up a pretty good bag. The tiger had been tied on a pad elephant, and arrived at Shikargurh before the hunters, who were met some way from the house by Mr. Besborough.

"What is all this I hear," said he, "about shooting tigers on foot. Surely, Campbell, you were not such a griff as to do so, especially with this youngster (pointing to Hampton) under your care."

Campbell expressed his deep regret, but excused himself on the score of his not thinking the tiger was on land at all, and after a few more remarks the subject was dropped.

Mr. Besborough seemed unwilling to go after any large game for a day or two, so Hampton had an opportunity of trying his skill with the fowling-piece on snipe, wild duck, and other water-fowl which swarm in Bengal during the cold weather. The ladies of the party made the afternoons and evenings pass away pleasantly, with billiards, music or dancing, and Hampton felt almost sorry that his lot had

not been cast among the planters, who seemed to lead such
a jovial life.

One morning, when the elder sportsmen seemed disin-
clined to hunt, and Mr. Besborough had some business to
settle, the younger guests proposed to take out all the dogs
they could muster, and have some amusement on foot in a
neighbouring village, which was of great extent and had
heavy coverts round it. Coolies with spades accompanied
them to dig up any jackals or other vermin which might be
found, and double-barrel fowling-piece in hand, the light-
hearted boys started. " Keep a bright look out for snakes,"
said one of Hampton's companions, "we are very likely to
come across some to-day, especially if we stumble upon any
old ruins, so beware of putting your feet or hands into any
suspicious-looking holes." The dogs, belonging to a dozen
different masters, were of all breeds, from the little skye
terrier to the big mastiff, and the amount of fighting,
yelping, and snarling which ensued when they were let
loose, was appalling. " What on earth are we expected to
hunt with this extraordinary pack ?" said Hampton. " Oh,
nothing in particular, and everything in general," replied a
young fellow, who had been in the country a few months
only, "the great fun is, that you never know what may
turn up. It may be a thundering ' cobra capella,' a
jackal, or the dragon of Wantley that the dogs tackle, they
are not fastidious, and as we do not know what strange
monsters the jungle contains, there is great excitement

when the dogs find anything." With some difficulty the pack is turned into the cover; masters follow; coolies begin to yell, dogs to bark, and the village resounds to the hideous din. There is a great amount of creeping under bushes, forcing their way through thorns, jumping over hedges and ditches, and altogether it is very warm work.

After a while there is a short silence followed by a great deal of scuffling about, and then the dogs seem to go mad altogether. The hunters rush to the spot as fast as creepers and thickets will allow, and find them collected under a bushy tree, which a few of the most eager attempt to climb, while some sit whining at its foot. No one could make out what was the cause of the disturbance, till a cooly forced his way through and examined the tree, and there, trying to hide himself on a branch, was a large brindled tiger-cat. These are formidable opponents to a dog single-handed, but of course would have no chance against a pack. After several unsuccessful attempts to dislodge the animal, a couple of barrels of small shot send him flying into the air, and the dogs soon finish him when he reaches the ground. Again they are urged on, and this time the barking is varied every now and then by a sudden cry of pain. One little skye terrier runs up to Hampton with his tail between his legs and whining piteously. On stooping down to examine him, he finds a porcupine-quill stuck an inch or so deep into his shoulder. After relieving the poor little fellow, Hampton pushed forward, and there, with his back arched and every quill quivering on end, stood the irate animal. The dogs were in a frantic state round him, at a respectful distance, however, for no sooner did they approach than they met with the same reception as the little skye terrier. The coolies, having an eye to a delicious roast, begged the gentleman to make him over to them, which was readily agreed to, as the dogs were unable to close with their bristling enemy. They were now whipped off, and made for another part of the village, near which was an old tank. After a while the dogs seemed to have found something particularly exciting, and this time the din is perfectly unearthly.

The youngster who had jokingly referred to dragons, now shouted out, "Here he is at last, Templemore, spikes and tail all complete."

Hampton ran up, but started back at the hideous appearance of the creature before him. It was a large guana, which, with tongue protruding and hissing loudly, was making short charges at the dogs. He was seven feet long, of a yellowish green colour, and seemed the link between the lizard and the alligator.

CHAPTER VIII.

THE CIVILIAN'S HURDLE RACE—BOAR HUNTING—ALLI-
GATOR FISHING—CALCUTTA BOTANICAL GARDENS.

AFTER gazing their fill at the strange monster mentioned in our last, he was left to the tender mercies of the coolies, who doubtless cut him up and ate him at their evening meal. The pack was called off, cigars were lighted, and with torn clothes and dust-begrimed faces, our huntsmen wended their way home.

The account of their adventures made Mr. Besborough laugh not a little.

"You will soon tire of such vermin killing," he said to Hampton, "but I used to be very fond of it myself when I was a boy, and many a strange adventure I have had when hunting on foot. I am surprised you did not come on a leopard, as there are some in the village you were in to-day, and if you had met one, a few of the dogs would have been finished to a certainty."

Next morning was to be our hero's first experience of hog-hunting, and his anxiety as to his own capabilities was

not a little raised, when he heard of the prowess of the wild
boar of Bengal.

"Where do you intend to go ?" asked one of the guests
of his host after dinner.

"Well," he said, "I am not very sure, but I think the
Hurree Shunker jungle will be the best. A good deal of it
is burnt and cut down by this time, and we may have some
decent riding ground. Last year we went there too early,
and could do nothing."

Their host's motion was agreed to, and great was the
speculation as to the first spears that would be ridden for,
and the amount of disabled horses or riders there would be.

Hampton suited himself with a nice light weapon from
Mr. Besborough's armoury, and begged him to let him have
the same horse he had ridden before.

Mrs. Besborough was very unwilling that he should run
any more risks, after his dreadful encounter with the tiger,
but she was laughed out of her fears, and he promised to be
as careful of himself as he possibly could.

Next morning saw a gallantly mounted party cantering
gently to the jungle, to which the elephants had been sent
before day-break. The cover which was to be beaten by
them consisted for the most part of reeds, through which
they forced their ponderous bodies, bringing down large
masses to the ground. The crashing noise mingled with
their shrill trumpeting, was more than the pigs could stand,
and they began to run about in all directions, charging

through the line. At last a fine boar broke in front of the horsemen. "Tally ho" was the cry, and they bound madly across the plain.

The boar was a very fast one, and led them at best pace over some very bad ground, in which the cut reeds stuck up like spears, and it was lucky that he was not brought to bay in this, or many a fine horse would have been injured.

Hampton was a light weight, and was in the front rank of the riders. Gradually he found that he was creeping ahead of the others. Taking a good pull at his horse's head he urged him on gently but firmly. The noble Arab answered to the call, and gained on the boar. A few more yards and the first spear is his ; but not only must you ride well, but you must have a practised hand, or you miss your blow, and till blood is drawn the spear is not won. Hampton wondered, as he closed on the boar, why he did not charge, and when, at last he did, it was so suddenly, that the spear glanced over his back. The Arab bounded in the air, jumped right over him, and thus saved himself, but Hampton had lost the prize. He now took a pull at his horse to see how the others got on. The next nearest hunter was an experienced hand, and as he was charged, buried the spear deep between the boar's shoulders. He now stood at bay, and another novice, who, like Hampton, had come from Calcutta, and was splendidly mounted on a very impetuous English mare, rode like the wind at him. They met. Instead of gently holding out his spear, he waved it in the air and dashed it, as he thought, into the boar, but, alas, his want of skill and his flurry, made him lose his aim; the leaded spear, slightly over-balanced, went right through his own leg above the ancle, and with a shriek of pain, he fell headlong on the ground.

Besborough and the rest of the party were now after another boar, and Hampton, with one or two who were near him, took care of their wounded companion.   Luckily among the sportsmen there was a medical man who tied up the injured leg, and the patient was taken home by him on one of the elephants.   Hampton then galloped on to see if he could not have one more chance, and luckily for him, as the second boar doubled, he came quite close to him.   He was now more cautious, and as the animal slightly slackened his pace preparatory to his charge, he leaned a little over to the right, poised his spear, held his horse well in hand, and at the exact moment turned him aside while he delivered his blow.

"Well done, Templemore," shouted Besborough, "you'll be as good a rider as your uncle in time."

This boar had been slightly wounded before, so that Hampton could not claim his spear, but he was very well satisfied with his performance on this his first day.

The third animal which broke cover was a small but very nimble one, and none but the younger members of the party thought it worth their while to ride him.   Hampton, of course, followed, and here, for the first time, came to

grief. As he was racing along neck and neck with another
light weight, he suddenly felt, as Marcus Quintius Curtius
must have done when he jumped into the chasm. His horse
sank from under him, he felt a tremendous shock, and turned
a somersault over his head. He had fallen into a pit used by
sugar-cane crushers to put their mill in. It was about ten
feet in diameter and some five feet deep, luckily it was
covered with long silky grass, which broke the horse and
rider's fall, and excepting a little sprain of his left shoulder,
our hero was none the worse.

His charger scrambled out of the hole and stood quiet
as a lamb till Hampton mounted him, and then rather
crestfallen walked him gently to where the main party were
assembled.

" Well, Templemore ; you've been down I see," said his
host ; " Not hurt, I hope."

Hampton explained how his mishap had occurred, and
making a temporary sling for his arm, joined Mr. Besborough
and some others in riding quickly home, that gentleman being
anxious to know how it fared with his Calcutta friend. Some
of the hunters remained on the field, and five boars were
killed, which was considered not a bad morning's sport.

What with hunting, love-making, and good fellowship of
all kinds, the hunting week at Shikargurh passed by only too
quickly for the generality of those to whom such golden
hours were, alas ! not likely to come round again for many a
long day. The best of friends must, however, part, and things

were packed up, and meetings for the future concocted preparatory to the final breaking up of the meeting. All thoughts
of sport had given way to sad and silent regrets, when just as
the batchelors were preparing for dinner, in walked Besborough
amongst them, and asked them to defer their departure for a
day, and join him in a fishing party, on a grand scale, next
morning. Every one of course volunteered, and their host
explained the matter.

"You see, I have a large fishery in the Nebis Khally Lake,
and this year, a rascally man-eating alligator has got in from
the Ganges, and after eating all the fish, by George, he is
trying his hand on the poor villagers. They have been to
me an hour ago, and report one man, a woman, and a child,
as having fallen victims already to the greedy brute. They
say also that he watches at the principal bathing places, and
no one dares to go near the water. What say you to try and
catch him alive ? I have had a proper hook and line made
and we can go to-morrow and spend the forenoon in trying to
rid the country of such a pest. We might shoot him, but
they say he is very wary, and we could not fire indiscrimi-
nately in a place surrounded by villagers."

After an early breakfast, a motley group of ladies, gentlemen, natives of all sorts in a variety of costumes, on horses,
elephants, and in toujons (open chairs), start for the lake,
which is really a beautiful one, and deserves description. At
some remote period it had been a reach of a large river, but as
is the history of all such places in Lower Bengal, the alluvial

deposit borne down by the Ganges had raised the whole country, and turned the river into a series of lakes. The luxuriant vegetation of the tropics soon changed the banks from a barren waste to thickly wooded scenery, and the now flourishing villages have brought with them the fruit-bearing mango and graceful tamarind. The peepul and banian hang over its banks, throwing a deep shade on the clear sweet water, forming numberless bowers where the much-guarded Hindoo maiden may bathe unseen. The cooing of the plaintive turtle-dove vies with the notes of the coqueel, the bird of Indian lovers, while the loud tap of the woodpecker surprises the European, who may never have heard its magical performance.*

A shady spot is selected for the ladies on the banks of the lake, where they can see some of the sport, and the gentlemen leave them awhile to go and superintend preliminaries. A live goat is to be the bait used to attract his alligatorship, and the hook is attached carefully to its side by numerous fine strings. To the hook is joined, not one rope, but for the first yard, about fifty pieces of twine, which cannot be bitten in two, as they separate when the teeth close on them. To the twine is added some sixty yards of thin rope, and lastly a large plantain tree is attached as a float, so that if the alligator takes to deep water his whereabouts can always be guessed by the tale-telling tree.

* This little bird can be heard on a still day for, I should say, a mile or more.

All the tranquillity and charm of the spot had been rudely disturbed by the advent of the much-dreaded alligator, and even the apathetic Bengalee was thoroughly roused to a sense of the unpleasantness of the situation. Besborough and his party soon reach the spot where their game lies hid. The goat is brought up, squalling most plaintively, and is attached to the hook. A native fisherman quietly glides down the bank, takes all the fishing apparatus into his canoe, and paddles noiselessly to the opposite shore which is the most unfrequented. The goat still keeps up his unavailing remonstrance, and as it reaches half way across the lake, say two hundred yards, one of Besborough's servants hurriedly touches his shoulder, and points with starting eyes to a black spot in the water. His master sees it, and with a quiet " Hush, gentlemen; no talking," they all lie down, peering over the bank with breathless attention. There, sure enough, are six inches of his forehead and his two protruding eyes. How he heard the goat from under water I know not, I relate the fact as it happened; but it was evidently its bleating which brought him from his lair. After a minute's survey he sinks again out of sight. The fisherman reaches the other bank, coils his line on the trunk of the plantain tree, pegs down the goat near the water, and paddles away down the lake. Besborough and his friends strain their eyes almost to blindness, watching for the slightest sign of a "bite," but the sun rises higher and higher, and they are still watchers.

A little more patience is generally agreed to when again one
of the eagle-eyed natives whispers, "There he is, to the south
of the goat." Many of the party could hardly make out the
little black object pointed to, amidst the drift wood and
other flotsams and jetsams which the wind is taking over to
that side to-day, but they are not long in doubt. Creeping
silently as the lizard does on to the fly, he closes to within
springing, or rather rushing, distance of his victim. A
splash of water, a faint sound of snapping teeth, and the
goat is gone as if by magic. In a few minutes the water
parts at the same spot, and the now triumphant monster
drags half his body on the shelving bank, with the dead goat
hanging from his mouth like a tassel. A dozen fierce
shakes, a wide opening of the jaws, and down goes master
Billy like a pill. A rifle ball soon conveys the unwelcome
intelligence to him that his meal must be digested elsewhere,
and sinking back into the water, the frightened beast swims
away.

"Now we will see if he is hooked," said Besborough.

Coil after coil of the line glides into the depths, and,
hurrah! there goes the plantain tree, like a small frigate
majestically down the lake. Now there is no holding anybody.
Out of every creek and bay canoes laden with natives come
paddling across the lake. The women, forgetting their usual
painful mock modesty, come round the spot where they think
the alligator may be hauled on shore, some waddling along
with their little ones seated monkey-fashion on their hips.

" Kill him; tear him to pieces," is the cry, and the air resounds with the abuse heaped upon the public enemy.

A canoe draws up to the float, and laughing till his teeth
shine again, one of the fishermen shews the admiring spectators
by pulling the line, that it's all right *down there*, adding a
little pantomine of his own, expressive of the state of the alligator's stomach, by humorously rubbing his own. A gentle
pull suffices to bring him along to a shallow bay, where he is
quickly surrounded by double nets. The natives think he is
now safe, and as he throws his head and shoulders out of the
water, snapping terribly at the rope, one of the most coura-
geous sidles his canoe up and tries to plant a harpoon in his
head, but it bounds off as it would from iron. The alligator,
maddened by the blow, rears up and throws himself backwards
right across the canoe; out go the occupants head foremost
into the mud and water, and the alligator changes places with
them. After a little rolling and struggling he slips into the
water and dashes through the nets as if they were cobwebs.
Besborough sees that the white man must come to the rescue,
and orders the line once more to be pulled in. Again the
alligator touches the ground, and as he fiercely shakes his
head out of water, a rifle ball or two in the neck finish his
career. With one hissing roar he rolls over and is at once
dragged on shore by half a hundred excited villagers. He is
tied on bamboos, and taken to be shown to the ladies, and
from thence to Shikargurh. He is there cut open and in his
stomach are found some human bones, the bracelets of the

woman and child, a few turtles' heads, and the goat which he
had lately swallowed.   Great was the glee of all at the successful ending of their fishing party, and Besborough was
voted unanimously to be the king of all hosts, past, present,
or future.   The bracelets were sent home to England by one
of the ladies, to a relative, on whose drawing-room table they
are conspicuously displayed at the present day.

We must now leave Hampton Templemore to find his way
back to Calcutta, after bidding a reluctant adieu to his host
and hostess, and accompany Mrs. Templemore to the grand
hurdle race, which our readers may remember was talked of
at Mrs. Blandon's "At home."   It was not to be one of your
common-place affairs, got up by the poor young officers at
Barrackpore or Dumdum.   No, no! This was to be a much
more aristocratic thing altogether.   All the élite of the Civil
Service were expected.   The riders were to be young civilians.
Their jackets and caps had been got up by a committee of
ladies, (after a world of trouble and anxiety) regardless of expense.   They were of red, blue, yellow, green, and white silk.
But the startling characteristic of the costume consisted in
a broad ribbon of contrasting colour placed across the breast
in imitation of the order of the Bath or Garter.   The horses
were the property of civilians, and the very hurdles were made
of bran new mats.

Drawn up in dazzling array before the grand stand of the
Calcutta race course, might be seen the carriages of those
well-known members of the nobility, the Hogyns Mogyns,

10

the De Robinsons, the Flushingtons, the Toodaws, and last, though not least, Montmorency Struggles. This gentleman came up to Mrs. Templemore's carriage and shed a few beams of radiance on its occupants.

"Aha, Miss Templemore," he was pleased to observe, "glad to see you out so early in the morning; 'tis the only plan to preserve your roses. Hope I shall meet you at Mrs. Blandon's fête to-morrow. We shall have a charming race this morning. Sure to be well-ridden, as the men are all in our service. I must go and see them weighed. Good morning."

Some of the young ladies and their chaperones were in a state of ecstatic delight, laughing and joking merrily, till they found out that the Hogyn Mogyn girls, who led the fashion, were almost in tears at the thought of any of the "dear young fellows being ki-ki-killed," as Julia Hogyn Mogyn, (who stuttered a little) called it, and then sentiment became the order of the day.

The famous Mrs. Macaroon was there, betting dozens of gloves with everybody, and inflaming the hearts of the susceptible by the tender glances she threw on them. She had made three little attempts to run away from her husband, but being rather fickle, tired of the novelty, and managed to get back before that good man, (who was wholly absorbed in his new work "on the structure of the cockroach's wing") had missed her much, and as he seemed perfectly satisfied, it was only looked on as a little eccentricity on her part, except perhaps by the very strict portion of the community. At any rate, she was received into society.

Of course Conrad Daymer was present, and installed himself as explainer-general of the proceedings to Laura.

"You see there are six hurdles, Miss Templemore, three feet and a half high, and the horses have to go all round the course. The favorite is an English horse, but as he is heavily weighted, some of the little Arabs may beat him."

All the preliminaries of weighing, and saddling, and blowing of bugles, being finished, the riders emerged from the weighing enclosure and cantered down in front of the stand. The almost painfully scientific attitudes assumed by the would-be jockeys, were delicious. Their new buckskins must have been sown on to their limbs, their new boots were shiny as looking-glasses, and their new saddles and bridles were spotless. None of these gay cavaliers were *very* experienced hurdle-race riders, in fact, they had never done such a thing in their lives before. They were all very beardless, and at what might be called the curly and fluffy-whiskered age. A common observer might have been inclined to think that they had unusually slippery seats, and that on leaning forward as jockeys do, they looked very much inclined to clasp their horses round the neck ; but this view was only that of ordinary mortals. It must not be forgotten that these young men belonged to a service that could anything, and therefore why not ride hurdle-races, of course, why not ?

All eyes were strained to make out the different riders as

they formed in line. There is a great inclination on the part of two or three of the horses to start tail first, and young Hogyn Mogyn was once clasped in young De Robinson's arms when their steeds would jumble up together, but at last, yes! they are off!

They dashed past at full gallop. The first hurdle is a little way past the Stand. They reach it! Every young lady shuts her eyes and shrieks faintly. One was distinctly heard to scream out "Edward!" There is a tremendous melee, three of the riders are in front of their saddles, and the rest have their feet out of their stirrups or are going through some other little performance of the kind. There is a great deal of slashing of whips and sawing of horses' mouths, but not one horse has cleared the jump! This was an intolerable state of things. The riders *were gentlemen* although vain ones, and the hot blood mounted to their faces as they felt the eyes of the spectators burning holes in their gay silk coats. But it was no use, the horses were perfectly untrained, and had, moreover, found out that none of their masters could ride. Refusing a leap is a catching disease, and never proved more so than on this occasion.

Again and again an attempt is made, but only results in young Flushington being made to stand on his head in the most ignominious manner. Some of the gentlemen spectators, amongst whom were some really good riders, began to laugh. The Lieut.-Governor's carriage drove off. Others gloomily followed. *That hurdle race was never talked of in polite circles.* It was, we are almost afraid to record it, a *failure!* Only one horseman, goaded to desperation, got his steed over the first jump, and then flew pluckily over the rest. The others were nowhere.

Laura Templemore had seen Conrad nearly every day since his arrival in Calcutta, and the knowledge that he was likely to be a partaker of her pleasures, shed a lustre over things which otherwise would have been but common-place. Her aunt never now referred to Captain Desmond, and that gentleman seemed rather to avoid meeting her, since her candid avowal at Mrs. Blandon's. He had not, however, given up all hope, and trusted to the chapter of accidents to afford him an opportunity of some day gaining a place in her affections. He had spoken a few words to her at the hurdle race, expressive of the pleasure he would experience at the next day's fête at the Botanical Gardens, but he was in no way marked in his attention. A lover's quick eye could, however, see that there was something constrained in Laura's manner, as long as Captain Desmond was by her side, and Conrad felt the first pang of jealousy creep across his heart, when, on his questioning her, she blushed and hesitated slightly.

"Captain Desmond came out with me," she said, "and some of the ladies thought him handsome, but I do not like his manner, although he is, doubtless, very accomplished."

Conrad too thought him very good looking, and instinctively marked him out as his rival.

"You have not promised to walk in the garden with him

to-morrow," said he in a low tone as he leant over the side of the carriage.

"I have not," she replied, "but really, Mr. Daymer, I do not see why I should refuse to do so." She was piqued at Conrad's tone, and woman-like thought she would teach him a lesson. But alas, hers was but a very soft nature, and when she saw him turn away from her, she would have given a great deal to recall the petulant speech. He said no more, but, bidding the ladies adieu, walked away from the spot.

Laura drove home absorbed in thought, and had little heart to enjoy a visit to the different shops which her aunt had proposed to visit during the morning, although she could not help being amused at the strange contrast to those she had been accustomed to in England, presented by the Exchange, and the different millinery establishments where the beauty and fashion of Calcutta loved to spend their mornings. At the first of the above-named places, which is an *omnium gatherum* of every species of merchandise, our heroine noticed with surprise the durwans or door-keepers with their caste-marked faces, and on reaching the grand saloon which is up-stairs, instead of trim neatly dressed shopwomen, found it lined by natives dressed in turbans and white muslin robes who were ready to supply her wants whatever they might be. Many of these men were strapping moustached fellows, and the idea of asking them for some of the little articles which men are not supposed to know anything about, was so ridiculous, that she could not help laughing merrily. "My dear aunt, I cannot ask that fierce-looking man about the silk stockings I require, I cannot indeed, so if it must be done I leave the matter to you." "Oh," replied Mrs. Templemore, "poor Gunga Baboo is a most inoffensive man, and you will hear what capital English he talks. Here, Baboo, I want some silk stockings for the Miss Baba."

We are sorry we cannot do justice to the Baboo's English, but Laura could not help turning away every now and then, and laughing heartily, for the difference between the man's appearance and the subject of his conversation was so great that it was utterly absurd. In time Englishwomen become accustomed to natives, and treat them as if they were not men at all, but little do they know the real hearts of these cunning sycophants, and it is lucky that the remarks made by them about our unsuspecting countrywomen are not generally known. From the Exchange our friends drove to one of the French modistes in Chowringhee, which was not like a shop at all, but consisted of a suite of rooms in one of the large dwelling-houses of that aristocratic quarter, furnished with glass-covered cases in which were displayed ribbons and laces in charming array. The glass cases are, alas, a necessity, and not merely ornamental, in the damp climate of Bengal, for silks or ribbons if at all exposed, are ruined in a few hours, and woe be to the innocent English bride who lays in a store of gloves, for if they are not hermetically sealed they are of all the colours of the

rainbow in one week of the rains. Although it was the cold
weather season the sun became oppressively hot in the
dusty streets of the town, and our heroine was glad to find
herself on the road home, with the prospect of an hour or
two of rest in her own room, where she might think quietly
over the events of the morning.

"You look tired and pale, Laura," said her aunt, as they
drove home, "I must not keep you out in the sun shopping
so long, or we shall have you laid up with fever, and that
will never do during the gay season. You must to bed
early to-night, and be ready to enjoy yourself thoroughly
to-morrow."

In the evening she vainly looked for Conrad amongst
the riders on the strand, but he was not to be seen, and she
could not extend the hand of forgiveness which she had
intended to do at their very first meeting.

The morning of Mrs. Blandon's party proved a most
propitious one, and conveyances were to be seen leaving all
parts of the town at the appointed hour. The programme
of the route was as follows: Ladies and gentlemen were
to meet opposite the garden, and then to cross the river
in sundry pinnaces and bhauleahs, which were to be in
waiting. After the amusements of the day were over, all
were to re-embark, and float up with the tide in the evening.

The botanical gardens of Calcutta are situated in the
most beautiful part of Garden Reach, on the opposite side of
the river to the town. This is a great drawback, for the

Hooghly is at all times, and especially at the period of the freshes, a very dangerous river for boats. · The tides run at a tremendous pace, the stream is crowded with large ships, and to add to other bad qualities, the bore rushes up at the commencement of the flood, with racehorse speed.

Since the river has been so crowded and the primitive manners of the residents have been so much changed, parties to the gardens have nearly gone out of vogue, but at the time we write of, a few used to come off in the cold season. A more beautiful place could not be selected for a fête champetre, for here have been collected from all corners of the tropics, trees and flowers of the most fantastic or beautiful growth. Parties picnicked under the shady trees, as in England, with this slight difference that mighty tables were spread and chairs were used, while dancing was carried on in a covered room built for the purpose.

Laura was delighted to find Conrad ready to assist her to land, and to see that the shade which had been cast over him at their last meeting had passed away. Perhaps his bright face was only a reflex of her own, for she was indeed glad to be once more near him, with the prospect of a delightful ramble through the beautiful garden which presented to them so many strange objects of admiration. " You will walk with me, Miss Templemore, will you not ?" said her lover, and hardly waiting for an answer, he asked Mrs. Templemore's permission to take her niece on an exploring expedition. Neither of the youthful pair had seen ought of India that was repulsive.

To them the shady wood brought no thoughts of wasting fever; hidden to them was the deadly snake coiled up in yonder thicket. The brilliant sky could surely never change to the darkness of the storm-laden season, the balmy breeze had nothing in it to warn them of the scorching winds of the Indian summer.

Conrad only saw before him, beautiful and blooming, the lovely English girl with whom were associated all the tenderest feelings of kindred and native land. She looked up and felt that with him no place could be dreary, no situation trying. And thus in their own bright fairy land they wandered on, happy, thrice happy.

"Do you know, Miss Templemore," he said to her, "that I think India is peculiarly the country to bring out a man's better nature. We all feel that we are pilgrims in a foreign land, and surrounded as we are by the native population, cling to our own countrymen in a way not understandable by people in England."

Laura had indeed felt the truth of this remark, and could not help saying "Yes, and then only think how much more these feelings must be intensified in my case, who am an orphan, and who, should my uncle go home, would only have my brother to protect me. He too might be called away by duty, to places where I could not follow."

"Do not say, dear Laura, that you would have only Hampton as your protector, I pray you think of me as a second brother, as one who is ready to devote his every thought and action for your welfare, and will only be too well rewarded if you will deign some day, when he has deserved it, to allow him to call himself by a warmer, dearer title than even brother, your true, your loving"——

The sentence was stopped by a great puffing and blowing behind them, which announced Montmorency Struggles.

"I have been sent for you, Miss Templemore, by your aunt; we are all going to see some native Juggling under the banyan tree, and she begs you to come as quickly as possible."

Poor Conrad wished Mr. Struggles at the bottom of the Hooghly, but go they must. They therefore joined Mrs. Blandon and the other guests under the far-famed Banian* tree, which spreads over a large extent of ground, and being protected, is more perfect in its arcades of pendent trunks, than is generally the case in open villages where the cattle constantly browse on their soft rooted ends, and thus prevent them reaching the ground.

The Calcutta one is a very fine specimen, but there are some known only to a few old Indians, which would exhaust our vocabulary of superlatives if we tried to describe them. One is at Colgong, some two hundred and fifty miles north of Calcutta, and two others are in the district of Tirhoot. Under one of the last a fair is held. It is called "Kuttay Thacoor," from a shrine which is built under its central trunk, and

---

* There is no such native name as Banian. The tree is the Ficus religiosa, and is termed Butt or Burr in Hindostanee.

covers four acres of ground without a break. It is perfectly mushroom shaped, so intensely thick that a splendid shade is afforded under its green canopy on the hottest day, and the ground underneath is beautifully clean and free from undergrowth of any kind.

The jugglers whom Laura was called to see were of the wild race called Nutts, the gipsies of India.

CHAPTER IX.

INDIAN JUGGLERS—WRECKED IN THE HOOGHLY—
STRUGGLES PROPOSES.

In our last, our heroine had been summoned to witness the performance of a party of gipsies, who are generally acrobats and jugglers by profession. Their matted locks, large necklaces made of beads, shells, tigers' teeth, and other charms, gave them a particularly strange look. In real sleight of hand and dexterity they far excelled their European brethren of the magic art, having no aid from apparatus, clothing, or confederates, and yet they made eggs and stones and birds disappear and reappear in the most extraordinary manner, being surrounded all the time by a circle of spectators, and being nearly naked down to the waist. This party did not profess to be masters of some of the almost incredible feats which have been (truthfully or not) recorded of Indian wizards, but some of their displays were, we think, sufficiently startling, their peculiar excellence consisting in their being the results of long practice and unrivalled delicacy of hand and keenness of eye.

The first was called the " Cheerea-ki-shikar," or bird-shooting. One of the men balanced a wooden representation of a tree with ten branches, on his nose. He then placed an artificial bird on the end of a skewer with his hands, transferred it to his mouth, and with his lips and tongue only, stuck the bird on one of the above branches. He did this ten times, and then shook them about to show their perfect balance. He now dropped ten shots into his mouth, placed a tin spout between his lips, and without using his hands, knocked the ten birds off the ten branches, each with a single shot.

The sportsman now gave place to a performer with the sword. His first act was to send for a packet of the soft milky leaves of the native plant called the "Bhenda." These he counted, and muttered some incantation over, finally tying them up with a blade of grass into a roll. A boy was ordered to lie down flat on his back on the grass, and the roll was placed on his naked abdomen. The man now unsheathed a bright native tulwar, or scimetar, and with outstretched arm balanced himself over him. He waved the sword twice or thrice in the air, and then with a sharp cut brought it down on the leaves. The ladies were very much alarmed, and begged that this might be the last of this species of display, but the man only smiled, and took round the little packet to show that it had been fairly cut in two, while there was not even a mark on the boy.

A little girl now stepped forward and requested the audience to observe a novel way of stringing beads. She put a handful of these of the smallest description into her mouth, and then, holding a horse-hair between her teeth, began rapidly to thread them with her tongue and lips, each following the other to the knotted end of the hair, which hung to the ground.

The next trick demanded an immense amount of dexterity. A large top was spun in the air, and then caught in the palm of the hand, never having touched the ground. It was then transferred from the hand to the thumb nail, and from this to the end of a slip of bamboo, which bent into the segment of a circle. This was then balanced on the forehead, and the top was kept spinning for an indefinite time.

The entertainment closed by one of the women being enveloped in a cloth, which in a few seconds was withdrawn and discovered her seated in the air, over the point of a sword, the hilt of which rested on the ground. One of her hands leant on a stick, and this was the actual point of support, but the situation of the woman appeared so unpleasantly dangerous, that it had the effect of making all the ladies leave the spot rather abruptly. This trick was the only one in which apparatus was used, and the *modus operandi* is understood in Europe.

Numerous sources of amusement kept the company in an agreeable state of excitement till their appetite warned them that time was passing, and it was pleasant to see the unanimity of purpose displayed in making for the grove, in which the luncheon, laid out with enchanting elegance, invited all to come and approve. If they were merry from the combined influences of the cloudless day, agreeable society and

brilliant music, what were they after the iced champagne?
Montmorency Struggles was in his glory. He had found a
chicken " mayonnaise," which exactly suited his refined
taste. He had washed it down with imperial Clicquot.
Sweet Laura Templemore was sitting opposite to him.
Could life be viewed under a more charming aspect?

Reader, have you ever seen a large " cobra " fed with frogs?
With sparkling eye and arched neck, he gloats over his victim, and yet he seems stupid, for he gloats and gloats, but
delays his spring so long, that you get tired of him. We say
it with all due respect, but the look of Struggles and of the
snake were identical.

Laura felt a strange fascination creep over her when, ever
and anon, as her eyes involuntarily turned in his direction,
she saw he was staring still. She thought he meant something, and she was right. He was debating how he could
devour *his* froggy, that is to say, he intended to ask her to
walk with him, and then propose. But the proposal—there's
the rub. Was it to be business-like—this kind of thing—heart
and hand; thousand a year; settlement; carriage and jewels;
Miss Templemore; Madam —— ? Or was he to sink down
on his knees, and do the youthful lover? He was fearfully
perplexed. Suppose he was caught on his knees. He was
stout—suppose he could not get up again easily. The thought
made him perspire. He wiped his forehead. A glass or two
of champagne will set all right. It does and he advances to
begin the action.

Laura of course could not refuse to walk with him till the dancing commenced, and casting a serio-comic look at Conrad, who was sitting next her, she placed her hand on his paternal arm, and glided away. We shall follow. They sauntered on till they reached a very retired portion of the grounds, and after a few common places, which greatly relieved Laura's mind, her companion seemed suddenly to be attacked with a combination of bronchitis and asthma, and was painfully silent. She felt his arm tremble.

"Do you admire *very* young men?" he at last rather spasmodically asked. "Do you admire very young—inexperienced—foolish you know—boys, in fact, you know, Miss Templemore?"

Laura said she rather hated that class of the Queen's subjects.

"Ah!" he said, "I thought so; the late Mrs. Struggles thought so, and all sensible women do the same. You are aware, I dare say, my dear Miss Templemore, that I am very well off; rich in fact, you know; Company's paper, and all that sort of thing. I have a splendid place at Khosamudpore, and by Jove, (here his asthma left) my cook and khansumah *are* treasures. And yet I am unhappy—ahem!"—

It was Laura's turn now to be slightly asthmatic, and she coughed.

"Yes, I am unhappy (he seized her hand), very unhappy, unless you choose to make me otherwise, Miss Templemore. May I presume to call you *dearest* Miss Templemore? Will

11

you ?— that is to say, can you ?—in fact, may I have the honour ?—that is, will you marry me ? "

None of the trees fell down, the earth remained unopened, and yet Struggles had proposed!

Laura felt sorry for his false position. "Mr. Struggles," she said, kindly but firmly, " I appreciate the compliment you have paid me, but I can never marry you ! "

Still the trees retained their equilibrium, the earth trembled not, and yet Struggles was refused. He felt hot, then cold, and then hot again. With five lacs of rupees, a man in the prime of life (fifty), who had so often been complimented on his looks, *refused* by that chit—well !

"Madam ! " he said, with a state of deportment worthy of Mr. Turveydrop. "Madam, let us return to the dancing-room."

Laura was not a little agitated by the events of the day, and was glad to sit down by her aunt to recover herself. She wondered how she would receive the news, on their return home, of her refusal of Mr. Struggles, but her courage revived when she thought that Conrad would never desert her.

Captain Desmond, who was one of the party, but had rather kept aloof from Laura, now came and asked her to dance. He seemed in bad spirits, and she could not help observing the great change in his manner, and also that he looked haggard and ill. He only once spoke to her.

"I am afraid," he said, "the last time we met at Mrs. Blandon's, I must have displeased you by mentioning a subject which I ought to have refrained from alluding to, I deeply regret my mistake, and trust you will forgive me. If you ever think of Frank Desmond let it be, at least, with kindly feelings."

Laura was relieved, when he left her, and although she felt a certain womanly gratification in the interest which such a general favorite as Captain Desmond had evinced, yet with that feeling was mingled a sense of dread which some men seem to have a fatal gift of inspiring in women.

The dancing lasted till the evening; the guests were delighted with the fête, and mid jokes and laughter, embarked on board the different boats which were to take them back to town.

We may here mention that in former days Pinnaces, Budgerows, and Bhauleahs were universally used in going up country, and to all the stations of Bengal, which are generally situated on one of the numerous rivers intersecting that province. Steamers, wheeled carriages, and now the railway, have of course finished the career of these slow but comfortable conveyances, but at the time of our story, a few still lingered at the different Ghauts, and were generally in a terribly rotten and leaky state. Paint and putty will do wonders, however, and in the cold weather, the old tubs were made to look quite gay. The pinnaces were of ten to twenty tons burden, schooner rigged; the budgerows were something like the Lord Mayor's State Barge, and the bhauleahs similar in shape, only smaller.

Mrs. Templemore, with a few of her most intimate friends, took possession of the largest pinnace, called the *Monarch*, a big heavy old craft, which pulled four sweeps. Among her party were Conrad Daymer and Captain Desmond, who, with Laura and some of her young companions, had chairs on the upper deck or roof, while the elder ladies sat in the state cabin. The *Monarch* took the lead, and with a great splash-ing of oars and singing of native songs, the little fleet steered up the river with the flood tide, which was about half spent. The journey was only one of half-an-hour's duration ; the slow progress, therefore, of the boats was rather agreeable than otherwise, as it enabled those on board to see both banks of the river, with their picturesque villas and gardens, while every now and then they glided past some majestic ship, from the decks of which the duty-restrained officers looked over longingly at the merry company floating past them.

" This boat seems to answer her helm very badly," said Captain Desmond to Conrad. " We passed a great deal too close to that last buoy ; don't you think so ?"

Conrad assented, and they tried to explain to the serang, (native Captain) that he ought to steer better, but the advice was lost upon the man, and he seemed quite satisfied with the boat's performance. He knew perfectly well that it was a dangerous task to guide such an old broken-backed ark through the shipping, but native-like, he trusted to destiny more than to his own exertions. The Bengalees, moreover, are almost amphibious, and the matter of swimming a mile or two is nothing to them; they are therefore perfectly reckless on their own rivers.

The boats had hitherto kept in the middle of the stream, but now had to cross to the Calcutta side. This involved threading their way through the ships, which were anchored closer and closer together. The rapid tide surged against the double chains of the heavy merchantmen, making the turbid waves rise a foot in front of their cutwaters. The *Monarch* pulled behind the stern of one vessel, and attempted to clear the bows of the next, but she was going too slowly to attain her object. It was evident, notwithstanding the frantic efforts of the boatmen, that she was dropping broadside on to the chain cable.

A cry arises from all, as they near the towering bows of the ship. Desmond and Daymer rushed to the sweeps, but it was too late; with one heavy roll, the ill-fated pinnace becomes firmly fixed on the chains. The tide now presses her till her old timbers crack again. They give way in a dozen places, and the water rushes into her hold and cabins. She is sinking! She falls over on her side; shrieks rend the air; the sailors from the nearest ships hasten to give their aid; the lighter boats of the party come to the rescue; and the ladies are torn out of the state cabin windows, some of them half drowned.*

"Where is Laura?" screamed Mrs. Templemore. "Oh, save her!" she said to a fine young fellow who had let him-

* This incident happened some years ago, exactly as it is narrated.

self down from the dolphin striker of his own vessel, (which they had struck against).

He jumped on board the wreck which was gradually settling under water, and at the risk of his own life searched every part of it; she was not there.

It was now seen that Desmond and Daymer were also missing. Some of the party pulled away with the tide in the hopes of finding some traces of the lost ones. The young sailor was first. What is that he sees ahead? Yes it must be; there they are! He shouts back, "They are saved, they are swimming close to the shore."

At the first heavy roll, after the *Monarch* struck, Laura and the other young ladies had been thrown over, but with the exception of herself, they all managed to cling to the rigging on the lee side. Desmond and Conrad were both rushing back from the sweeps, when they saw her fall into the water. They dashed after her, and being splendid swimmers, soon had her between them. Conrad felt his courage rise high, as he seized Laura's silken hair, and drew her head on to his shoulder with his right arm; Desmond had her round the waist with his left, and using one arm each, they manfully breasted the treacherous waves of that fatal river, and after a hard struggle with the eddies and under current, safely reached the shore.*

* Hardly a year passes without some one of the citizens of Calcutta being drowned. As to sailors and soldiers, they are lost by the dozen.

The boats with the other members of the party quickly gained the bank, and found the two young men chafing Laura's hands, to recover her from the faint she was in. They lifted her into Mrs. Blandon's carriage, who insisted upon Conrad and Desmond driving with Laura and her aunt, to her house, which was the nearest, while she made use of a friend's conveyance to bring the family doctor, with the least possible delay.

"You can have Blandon's things till your own arrive," she said, "so hurry home as fast as the horses can gallop."

After a few hasty adieus the rest of the party scattered in different directions.

Mrs. Templemore was almost beside herself, but as well as she could, with tearful eyes and trembling voice, thanked her companions for their gallant conduct. They begged her not to agitate herself, and said they should be well rewarded if Miss Templemore came to no harm.

They had only half-a-mile to drive, but the horses seemed to crawl, and all thoughts about themselves were lost in their anxiety to see Laura conscious once more.

Mr. Blandon, who had not been of the party, and had just returned from his office, was astounded to see four dripping figures come out of his carriage, one of them, as he fancied, a corpse; but he quickly comprehended the matter, and every one in a few minutes was made as comfortable as circumstances would admit. The young men explained the misfortune which had befallen the party, and while the carriage was again hurried off for their clothes, all waited anxiously for the arrival of Mrs. Blandon and the doctor. In a few minutes they came in, and the latter soon brought the welcome intelligence that Laura was fast recovering, although not well enough to thank her deliverers in person. Intelligence had also been sent to Mr. Templemore, and he arrived in hot haste to find things progressing favorably.

They had but a gloomy dinner that night at Mrs. Blandon's, and although she and her daughters tried their utmost to make their guests forget the terrible incidents of the day, all their efforts were unavailing. Every one's thoughts would recur to the dangers they had passed through, and then silence gradually stole over them.

Before Laura's deliverers left, Mrs. Templemore begged to see them again. She intended to say something more warmly expressive of her gratitude, more worthy of the occasion; but when they came up to her, looking pale and worn, her eloquence left her. She burst into tears, clasped their hands in hers, and feebly sobbed out, "Thank you, a thousand times, thank you."

What thought Conrad and Desmond as they lay on their sleepless couches that night? What a wide difference of feeling disturbed their rest! The first was all hope. His heart bounded with delight, as he exultingly said to himself, "Now I have shown myself her own true knight, she will surely believe in my deep, deep devotion." Then he pictured her drowning in that horrid river, while he was bound fast by

chains which he could not break. He tugged and strained
for bare life, to plunge in and save her, and then he woke
and sprang out of bed, glad to drive away the hideous nightmare, by pacing up and down hour after hour.

Desmond's mind was racked by a thousand conflicting
emotions. "I helped to save her life," he thought, "for
without me they never could have struggled against those
fearful eddies; but will this bring me any nearer my mark.
Will it make her love me?" Then a dark shade of the past
would spectre-like rise before him, and the hot blood coursed
through his brain, till like a raging maniac he paced wildly
up and down, almost unconscious of what he was doing.
After a while he collected his thoughts. "That boy, my
rival! I could quarrel with him easily enough; and then if I
shot him or he me, it would be gain either way." And yet,
no! Was woman ever thus won? His wide experience told
him never. Then came black despair, and he could hardly
keep his hands off his pistol-case, lying so temptingly near.
'Tis hard, that crossing of one's only real passion: that
snatching away of the idol, which has been worshipped with
a blind uncalculating faith. What if the report he had
heard before leaving England were true! What if that
wretched woman still lived! "No, no! she is dead!" and
he tried to laugh down his fears, but still the phantom would
rise before him. Suddenly the cool devil in his nature returned, and he calmed down, and then a little laudanum and
brandy did what tired nature refused to do; he slept.

The whole of Calcutta rung with the account of the accident, and when it was ascertained that Laura was in no danger, speculation was rife as to which of her deliverers she would reward with her hand. The gossips were, however, terribly disappointed when, after a few weeks of breathless expectation, our heroine's engagement was not announced.

In the mean time, Desmond had to join his regiment, which had gone up country, and Mr. Templemore was offered a judgeship some 400 miles from Calcutta, which he accepted. His wife, never a strong woman, was much shaken by the fright she had experienced, and as Laura also looked pale and delicate, it was resolved that they should go up to the hills to spend the hot weather. Mr. Templemore proposed to enter on his new appointment as soon as his wife left, and would be rejoined by her and Laura at the commencement of the cold weather, by which time the house, &c., would all be in good order.

Conrad Daymer had still some months to remain in Calcutta, to enable him to pass through the Civil Service College, which he hoped to accomplish in less than the usual time, as he showed great aptitude in learning the languages of Bengal.

Hampton Templemore had started from Calcutta as agreed on, shortly after his return from Kishnaghur, and without any incident worth recording, found himself at Allahabad, after five days of railway and dawk carriage travelling. An

unwonted number of ensigns were doing duty with the regiments at the above station, so having numerous companions,
he did not find the time hang very heavily on his hands. He
at once employed a moonshee, and after a good deal of rubbing
of the forehead and clutching at the hair, (by which great
mental perturbation is meant to be described) he mastered
the first difficulties of Persian and Hindostanee. After this
he found it plain sailing, and took a great interest in his
work. The Colonel and officers of his regiment were very
kind, and ready to put him in the way of managing properly
on his slender pay, and in this he was more fortunate than
the ensigns of the Queen's regiments, for these had no one to
give them advice, the colonels and officers being all griffs
alike.

Conrad Daymer had been constant in his attentions to
Laura, and had spoken to Mrs. Templemore and her husband
of his attachment to their niece. He was looked upon by
them as her future husband, but had not, however, formally
proposed to Laura herself, her reciprocation of his affection
being so apparent that he had almost forgotten the bounden
duty of every bachelor in this respect. He, however, made
amends for his remissness in the following manner. Before
she was thoroughly recovered from the effects of the shock
she had received, he used to spend his leisure hours in reading
to her, or sit talking of olden times on the terrace overlooking
the river. On one of these occasions, their conversation
strayed from one subject to another, till they began discussing

the marriage and domestic economy of a young couple whom
they knew—the Bartletts.

"Well," said Laura, "I cannot agree with you in thinking
she has shown great taste in furnishing her house; you don't
mean to say that red and yellow form a nice contrast?"

"No, I don't exactly mean to say that, but then I firmly
believe the unfortunate mixture of colours you talk of, is the
work of that vulgar fellow Bartlett; you can always tell him
a mile off by his waistcoat and necktie; and it is about the
only mistake in the house. I am sure you will never allow
me to interfere in that way," said Conrad, warming with the
subject, but totally forgetting that he had not yet received
permission to use the word "we."

"Oh, indeed, Mr. Conrad, what do you mean," said Laura,
her eyes dancing with mischief, "you have not yet informed
me by what right I should exercise any control whatever in
your domestic arrangements. I am really quite surprised at
your language."

"Then you are a sweet little humbug, that's what you
are," and [here turn away your heads, young ladies] he gave
her a kiss, then laughingly dropping on one knee, said,
"Angelic Miss Templemore, will you deign to accept the
homage of your devoted slave, and some day condescend to
arrange his drawing-room furniture?" after which [we are
only recording the truth] he kissed her again a dozen
times.

In a few days more Mrs. Templemore broke up her establishment, for the hot weather was creeping on, and the journey to Mussooree would take at least fifteen days, so sending their heavy luggage on first by steamer, our friends made ready for that not over pleasant trip for ladies, a journey by dawk.

The worst part of the undertaking, as far as roads were concerned, was accomplished by railway, which extended at this time to a place in the coal districts, some hundred and twenty miles north of Calcutta, called Raneegauge.

Mrs. Templemore had friends or acquaintances at many of the stations on their route, so was enabled to travel much more comfortably than those who were not so fortunate. They rested at Burdwan, Shergotty, Benares, and Allahabad.

Here of course they were met by Hampton. He was looking well, and talked of "my regiment," and was great about parades, drilling, &c. He "chummed" with another ensign, and was very proud and delighted to show Laura over their little dwelling. When Mrs. Templemore said that she would come and breakfast with him next morning, he and his friend nearly lost their heads altogether. Their two khidmutgars, who had only lately been promoted from mussalchees (plate washers), became so excited that they smashed half the crockery which Hampton had borrowed from the Colonel to do honour to his guests, and for fear of the consequences, bolted next morning across country, and were never seen again.

After a few days spent together, brother and sister had

again to part, with the hope, however, of meeting after the hot season, when Mrs. Templemore would return through the station, en route to their new home at Neelapore.

To those of our readers who have never been in India, it may not be uninteresting to know that there was only one land and one water route from Calcutta to Allahabad. The former was called the Grand Trunk Road, and was traversed in primeval days by the heart-sick traveller in a palanquin. As far as it went it was a blessing (the road we mean), but when you consider that most of the rivers were unbridged, the jungles teemed in places with tigers, the dawk bungalows, or resting places, were comfortless little thatched cottages, no aid obtainable from any European for sometimes a hundred miles, and in the hot weather great danger from fever, dysentery, or cholera, it was enough to make one shudder to think of unprotected women being sent such a journey, and yet it was done every day.

After many years, the ordeal by palanquin gave place to the lesser one by dawk carriage. This conveyance was not at all unlike one of the former abominations enlarged, and placed on four wheels. They were very strong, their roofs and walls being adapted to carry luggage and nick-nacks of all kinds.

To the humorous mind there was a fund of amusement in this mode of transit, and as in the course of ten years we only heard of one coachman being killed, a syce, or groom, having both legs broken, one gentleman an arm ditto, and of another losing one of his ears (an extraordinary case to be sure), it may be considered that a special providence protected the traveller through the perils of this method of locomotion. The fun we have alluded to was to be found chiefly in the horses—save the mark! Three to five pounds was the price paid for the best of them—need we say any more? They were generally ponies or galloways, vicious to such an extent that when in process of being conquered by the superior malignity of the demons who drove them, their performances became laughable.

The whole affair of harnessing and starting was a stand up fight, ending usually in the equine side being hit in a very soft place by some stupendously knowing dodge, when he gave in, and then he galloped like, well! I have no comparison except Mazeppa's horse, or one driven by a drunken Irishman after a fair. Fortunately the road was pretty straight, and though above the level of the surrounding country, the chances were so far diminished of being carried right off it. But in the hills the risks run were really appalling. It was the common practice to dash down a mile of steep declivity, sometimes with a sharp turn, ending in a bridge over a ravine fifty feet deep. Horses have been found in such places hanged in their own collars, from having jumped over the parapet, and an instance of this happened to a friend of the writer a few years ago. Sometimes when the horse was tired of galloping he used to shy off the road, and then there was an upset or a concussion against the first tree in the

track. In either case, but especially in the former, the traveller found himself in the midst of the mere wreck of his
former grandeur. He was generally bathed in a mixture of
Allsopp's beer, soda water, Eau de Cologne, and hair oil, and
was lucky if the guava jelly had not been upset into his best
hat or box of five hundred cigars.

As a case in point, we will narrate what happened to young
John Brown, of the uncovenanted service. He had persuaded,
not to say entrapped, his revered maternal parent into
going to Mussooree. This lady had a perfect horror of
horses. With her they were a species of supremely vicious
tigers, who had drunk of the concentrated essence of hatred
to the human race. She would only consent to travel by day
—slowly! Well! as slowly as bribes and entreaties could
accomplish, for remember, kind reader, that the horses had
only one pace and that was a gallop. She travelled in one
carriage with a daughter, her son following in another to
watch over their safety, and literally to pick up the pieces if
necessary. Judge what must have been his feelings, when he
saw that vehicle, containing all he loved and all the provisions
and crockery, with a black ayah and six tin boxes on the roof,
rush off the road, reel, go on two wheels, and disappear down
a slope into a grove of mango trees. We will draw a veil
over the sequel, as novelists say.

The above is one view of Dawk travelling.

Take another. At one of the halts you may be drinking a
glass of ale or lighting a cigar, or stooping forward to get

something out of the well, or feeding the baby from a bottle, or a hundred similar things, when that Roman-nosed pony which has been torn by main force from its stable, rears as it is harnessed; bounds forward just one yard and then stands *stock still*. Think what becomes of that foaming beverage, or how nearly your eye is put out by that lighted stick, or what a blow your nose may get, or how far down that devoted infant's throat that bottle may go, and agree with us in thinking that they were fools who had such an experience twice—*once* was the *common* lot.

CHAPTER X.

MUSSOORFE ; THE CAPTAIN'S WALL ; ROSA MARTINE.

LAURA and her aunt experienced some of the inconveniences
of dawk travelling mentioned in our last chapters, but they
were greatly modified by judicious halts, and very often by
the assistance of the police who had orders from the different
magistrates, in whose jurisdiction they might happen to be,
especially to protect their friends. They rested at the great
military station of Meerut for two or three days, and were
then about a thousand miles from Calcutta—ninety more and,
hey presto ! the hot, dusty plains of the Gangetic valley
change into the smiling Eden of Dehra Doon, (which lies at
the foot of the hills), and a little further on into the cool,
cottage-dotted, snowy-mountained, gay, delicious, Mussooree.

At Dehra, Laura, for the first time since leaving England,
saw the roses clustering over the roadside garden gate, and
heard the ripple of the clear mountain stream which supplies
the town with water. This is led on to a turreted reservoir,
from which it falls in tiny cascades, and is surrounded by an
ever changing group of picturesquely-clad natives who come
here daily to bathe.

Mussooree itself rises abruptly from the valley, having some seven thousand feet of elevation in a distance of only six miles. The ascent, therefore, in some places is very precipitous. One of the peculiar features of this sanatarium consists in there being no intervening range of hills to destroy the view of the plains, which, on a clear day, appear spread out as on a map for hundreds of miles, south, east, and west. The white-washed houses of Roorkee, the great engineering depôt, and even those of Meerut, ninety miles off, being sometimes visible to the naked eye. Large rivers, reduced to the semblance of ribbons of a pale straw colour, can be traced in all their wind-ings till lost in the extreme distance, being marked distinctly against the light green shade of the cultivated land, or the darker hues of the forest. In the hot weather it is a wonderful contrast to turn from this scene, quivering in the mirage caused by the fierce sun and burning hot winds, to the cool north, where ranges upon ranges of mountains are bounded by the awe-inspiring regions of eternal snow, from which the cool breeze blows so refreshingly, bringing down the ther-mometer, even in May, to 60°. Nor do comparisons cease here, they are offered in almost everything animate or inani-mate. On our right hand will be a fair hillman clothed in blanketing, with a creel full of wild apricots, or, perhaps, a pottle of blackberries (real English-looking blackberries) for sale, while on our left stands, patiently, a dark Hindustanee of the plains, lightly clad in muslin, who insinuatingly offers his luscious mangoes or rich ripe plantains. On the road before us two little gynee bullocks (about three feet high) are creeping along with their tiny load of lime, which they have doubtless brought up some break-neck path; while stalking majestically past them, is that long-legged, high-humped braminee ox of the plains, laden with two large skins of water from the nearest spring. The native market is supplied with all the usual Indian vegetables mingled with the products of Europe. The most delicious peaches are grown in the the Dehra valley, and Orleans plums of a coarse description can be bought for a shilling a hundred-weight; strawberries too at six anas a seer, or fivepence a pound. These may seem uninteresting details, but who that has lived for years in the tropics will not understand the delight of even *looking* at English fruit or flowers? Among these last the dahlia blooms conspicuously in the gardens of the residents, and the surplus roots having from time to time been thrown out here and there over the hillside, they now grow in sheets of glowing colours.

It is a strange feature of the Himalayahs at Mussooree, that properly speaking there are no valleys, by which we understand a plain between two hills. One range rises after another in a never varying series of steep ascents or tremendous precipices, beginning in a narrow ravine and ending in a sharp ridge, which generally runs east and west, the prevailing direction of these mountains for two thousand miles. On one of these ridges are scattered the villas and cottages of Mussooree, while towering seven hundred feet above is Landour, the military sanatarium. At the junction of the two stations stands the native bazaar. The crest of the ridge is here not more than thirty yards across, having on each side a precipice a thousand feet deep. The shops on both sides of the street actually hang over the abyss (being here and there propped up on poles) and appear in an awfully precarious position. As we leave the bazaar behind and proceed westwards the ground available for building becomes more extensive, the southern face of the mountain is less steep and every little shelf is appropriated for houses. Now and then a spur runs out, and these are all dotted with picturesque dwellings.

The whole had originally been thickly wooded with the oak and rhododendron, but with the most culpable want of foresight, these were nearly all cut down for firewood, the result being that the gravelly soil was left unprotected from the action of the rain, often causing landslips and consequent loss to the householders. An instance of this once came under the writer's observation.

A family, consisting of a very timid lady and her daughter, rented a pretty cottage, the proprietor of which had scooped and blasted the hill side till he had obtained sufficient room to build it. In doing this he had created quite a precipice below the next property, which belonged to an invalid and irascible officer, who had planned and erected for himself, as he thought, the perfection of a residence. A rainy season passed, and the gallant captain found that the earth of his little garden was being gradually washed down on to the roof of his neighbour's kitchen, which, Indian fashion, was detached from the house. He would often stand on the edge of the gulf, some fifty feet deep, and as he mournfully looked down the kitchen chimney, meditate on what he should do. One day a bright idea, clouded however by visions of the cost, crossed his mind. He must spend another five hundred rupees, and build a stone wall right up the face of the scarp. His neighbour who had caused the dilemma, made him a present of the materials, of which he happened to possess a store. The wall rose rapidly. It looked stupendously imposing. It was a labour of love for the captain to superintend it.

"You shan't have any more of my garden soil down into your place," he used triumphantly to say to the landlord of the "Acorns," as the cottage below him was called, "I think I have put a stop to *that*."

When it was finished, all his visitors were taken to admire his *chef d'œuvre*.

"There!" he exclaimed, "That's the style of wall you ought to build up here. None of your rubbishing affairs, but a regular business-like bit of masonry. Cost me five hundred rupees!"

Alas for all human projects; how often do they not fail! The rains commenced; the captain had neglected to carry the roof drippings of his house clear of the new wall. It stood out, however, bravely for a while. One day the timid lady was writing a letter; her daughter sat by her side plying the swift crochet needle. Their thoughts were calm;

the day was rainy but serene.   Nothing had lately happened
to frighten them—no storms, no lightning, no desperate
young ladies scrambling their ponies over breakneck places,
no nerve-shaking hillmen balancing themselves across dangerous ledges.

"Thank goodness, Emma," said the lady to her daughter,
"I am becoming more accustomed to the dreadful precipices
and other horrors up in these wild mountains, and I hope
there will be nothing to make me nervous again for a long
time," when crash!—rumble!—thud!—bang!—down came
the whole of the famous wall!

It was at the back of the house.   The cause of the commotion could not be seen from where the ladies were seated.
The mother thought the world had come to an end, and
fainted off dead in her arm chair, while the daughter rushed
to the verandah in time to see the servants creeping out of a
small side window of the kitchen, on which the avalanche had
fallen, covering it over, and hermetically sealing its doors and
windows, while the captain stood on the edge of the ruins,
surrounded by his wife and family, and waved his arms wildly
in the air.

The cottage taken for Mrs. Templemore was called "The
Oaks."   It was embosomed in a grove of the trees after which
it was named, and perched on such a small spot, scooped out of
the mountain side, that you could have jumped from Laura's
accustomed seat down hundreds of feet without a break, while
at the back of the house, their next neighbour, being nearly

straight over head, could have annihilated them by dropping a rock or two on their thatched roof. It was in a bay between two little spurs of the hill, and thus shaded and slightly darkened except at mid-day, you could look down on the plains sweltering in the rays of the fierce Indian sun, while (strange contrast) everything around was cool and calm and beautiful.

Laura never tired of looking at that wondrous scene, it seemed so much more like some artificially produced effect of the cunning scene-painter, than anything in nature. Then the cuckoo would come and sit quite close, and make the echoes answer to its clear, time-marked notes. To Laura they sounded mournfully; they drew her thoughts to child-hood, to Conrad and Hampton, to her father's and mother's graves (now only a comparatively short distance away), to her deliverance from the dread waters, and then she would weep, and pray to God to preserve those whom she loved so well.

The cottage had only four rooms and two dressing rooms, was thatched and had green windows and Venetian doors, with a verandah on three sides. This was made into quite a bower by the roses and honeysuckles, which were twined all over it, there being no danger in the hills from snakes or other creeping things.

The hill which bounded the view on the left was the famous Purree Puhar, or Fairy's Mountain. It was wooded up to the summit, in the centre of which might be seen the remains of what had been a large house. To the mountaineer the hill was haunted, and rash was he considered who ventured within its spirit-peopled boundaries after nightfall. A wild romantic tale was connected with the blackened walls, 'which stood out clearly in the bright sunlit atmosphere, and the natives, as they passed within sight of them, would shake their heads and whisper to each other "The fairies are generally powerless against the white man, but this time they have shown their might indeed."

The story ran thus—Rosa Martine was the eldest daughter of an officer, to whom promotion had crept with even more laggard steps than it generally does to the moneyless soldier. A large family had kept him poor, and it was only by exchanging into regiments serving in India, that he managed to struggle on with his captain's pay. Rosa, his pet, had been sent to England, where some kind relations had educated her for a merely nominal sum. At seventeen she returned to her parents and to her shabby home. After dreaming, as children will dream, of all kinds of luxury and pleasure which she was to enjoy in India, the reality of course proved doubly vexatious to her, and being a fine-looking girl, she experienced great mortification in not being to make as good an appearance as her young companions at the station. Among the officers of her father's regiment was a lieutenant of the name of Annerly, who interested Rosa more than any of the other young men who danced or flirted with her, and who, in his quiet modest way, showed that he had the deepest regard for her. Unfortunately, although a man of good family he was very poor. When, therefore, he proposed for Rosa's hand, his suit was rejected by her father, who would not entertain the idea for a moment.

"You see," he said to his daughter, "what poverty has brought my home to, take warning by my fate, and let not its curse follow you."

Young Annerly felt the disappointment bitterly, and obtaining leave of absence, started for England.

Rosa, as is usual with pretty girls in India, had several offers from men much her senior, and, persuaded by her mother and father, she accepted one of them Major Gorton, by marrying whom she gained wealth and luxury, but with them misery. Her husband, as many men had done before, thought he would have a pretty, easy-tempered plaything, when in fact he had secured a sneering, fretful, discontented wife, who seemed to think that title gave her a right to render his home miserable.

Some years passed away, and she became the mother of two children, as pretty as herself.

Her father's regiment had for some time been removed to a distance, and she had heard little of the movements of its different members, Annerly's name being purposely omitted in the letters received from her family. On an evil day she determined to spend the hot season at Mussooree. It would do her children good, and she would escape the daily quarrels with her husband. A pretty cottage was taken for her, and charmed with the climate and novelty of everything around her, she watched with delight the bright hue of health rise in her children's faces.

Separation and reflection on the folly of the life they had been leading, led both husband and wife to inwardly vow amendment for the future, and their letters grew kinder and more confidential than their personal intercourse had ever been. All promised well for a reconciliation, and Gorton looked upon that trip to the hills as a most fortunate occurrence.

It was willed to be otherwise. By some fatality, Annerly, who had long ago returned from England, had taken six months' leave, and gone up to Mussooree. Too late for his happiness, he had unexpectedly inherited a large fortune from a distant relative, and the once poor lieutenant was now rich. In the comparatively limited circle of a hill station, Rosa Gorton and her former lover were frequently thrown into each other's society. But what necessity is there to detail the usual incidents of such a story? Human passion, want of principle, and unlimited opportunity did their usual work of ruin. Her letters to her husband became less frequent. He grew suspicious, or perhaps some one gave him a hint or two, and suddenly he intimated his intention of visiting the hills. This severed the last link. Sending her children to a friend, she eloped. Major Gorton arrived almost immediately after her flight, called out his enemy, and was severely wounded in the encounter. A broken-hearted man, he returned to the plains with his little ones, intending to start for England, where he purposed to sue for a divorce as soon as possible.

Annerly and the wretched woman he had seduced were so shunned by every one, that he withdrew from the station, and rented the solitary house on the Purree Puhar. It was known to the hillmen that this and one or two of the neighbouring peaks were subject to be struck by lightning, (probably from the large quantity of iron ore contained in the rocks). The landlord had been dissuaded from building on such an exposed site, but he would listen to no one, and carried out his whim. The stormy season came on, and our two fugitives were installed in their new home.

" Their sneers cannot reach us here," Annerly would say to poor Rosa, and then he would swear to be true to her, and to marry her the moment he could legally do so.

One night the inhabitants of Mussooree were startled by a sudden blaze on the fairy's hill. They looked and wondered. In an hour or so a band of horror-stricken servants rushed into the station magistrate's compound, and breathlessly described what had happened.

The sahib and mem (lady and gentleman) had just retired to rest when a storm broke over the hill. One fearful flash of lightning was followed by a peal of thunder, which shook the walls of the house. In a few minutes the thatched roof burst into flames, and, by their account, their efforts to penetrate to their master's room had been unavailing, the fire and smoke driving them back at each attempt. Assistance was immediately sent from the station, but it was of no avail. It appears that the inmates had been struck by the lightning as they slept, and the house being burnt over them mattered little to the dead.

It has never been rebuilt, and its mouldering ruins are the only memorial of the unhappy pair, who were buried in a little garden adjoining.

A month or two of the invigorating climate soon restored Mrs. Templemore and Laura to health, and they were able to discard their jumpans (or Sedan chairs), and take long walks, or canter about on two little hairy ghoouts (hill ponies), which a friend had sent them from Almorah, another of the stations in the Himalayahs. They received letters daily from one or other of those they had left behind them, and as everything progressed well with their loved ones, their spirits rose, they forgot the trials they had gone through, and looked forward with happy longing to their meeting in the cold weather.

Mr. Templemore wrote in high spirits about his judgeship, and the district he was appointed to. He had secured a beautiful house, and hoped to have everything in order by October.

The last news from Conrad Daymer was most cheering. He expected to pass through the College in six months, and intended to apply for an assistant-magistrateship at (only fancy) Neelapore. This Mr. Templemore could easily manage for him, so he looked upon it as a certainty. His letters used to make Laura's thoughts wander to the future, and with one of them in her hand, she would lean back in her old seat in the verandah, and dream for an hour or two at a time.

There was no lack of gaiety at Mussooree. The fact of all being in one service prevented any difference of caste in the residents, and individual likes and dislikes, with disparities of age or fortune were the only governing elements of society.

The beauty of our heroine very soon attracted a host of butterfly admirers, who lounged by the side of her chair on the Mall, or rode with her round the " Camel's back," but she flirted with none of them, and was voted decidedly slow by all the lady-killers of the station.

" That girl Templemore is sweetly pretty," said young Wheedler to his friend Lispey as they sat in his room one day at the Himalayah Club, " Sweetly pretty!"

" Ah!" replied Lispey, " I should think so; but she has no heart, not a bit. She asked me—Why ? I wished a rose from her bouquet the other night,—and did it so naturally that hang me if I could tell her why, by Jove, I couldn't; and I'll tell you what, old boy, she's either a fool or engaged."

" Shouldn't wonder, now I think of it," said the other. " That's the reason she seemed so deaf one evening, when I asked her to walk in the moonlight after dancing with her. You know a fellow can ask a girl *tenderly in a whisper*, to walk in the moonlight, but when you have to repeat it out loud for the benefit of the bystanders, it is more than any fellow can stand."

After May the rains set in on the hills, and then the bright panorama which Laura had always spread out before her was hidden altogether by the heavy clouds. Not the least novel and beautiful of the sights at this season in the Himalayahs, are these wonderful evidences of an Almighty power which bring from the far off ocean their burden of moisture, and pour it out on those old giants, the high mountains, who catching the precious treasure in their out-stretched arms, pour it down again to mother earth, making her smile with cities and green fields. As each relay of clouds creeps slowly up from the plains, you mark their fleecy masses at first no bigger than your hand, plainly shewn against the wooded mountain side, thousands of feet below ; gradually they cover distant objects from the sight; now that rock, now yon trees, then the cottage which lies a few hundred feet beneath you. After a short interval the ob-server feels himself enveloped and the drops begin to trickle down the leaves and off the thatch of the verandah under which he is standing, while the cloud gently melts away in a soft shower.

No one cares much for the rain in the hills, a wetting not necessarily bringing on fever, or some other ailment, as it generally does in the plains. The ladies' chairs, too, are made with waterproof covers, and it is only in the event of being taken unawares while out riding, that they are likely to be inconvenienced.

The appearance of some of the gentlemen while paying a morning visit during this season, is decidedly ridiculous, elegance being completely sacrificed to comfort, and it is odd when you go out to welcome Colonel and Mrs. Wellington Buckram to find that proud warrior in a blanket round his waist, complete oilskin suit and dustman's sou-wester hat. The blanket, we must explain, being to keep the saddle dry.

Hampton's letters to Laura after the warm weather commenced were not so cheerful as they used to be.

"You see," he said in one of them, "it is not very pleasant just as you are really getting a little sleep to hear that confounded bugle and be half pulled out of bed by your bearer at four o'clock for morning parade. Then when the sun rises it gives us a tremendous headache, whenever we have to wear the wretched infantry shacko. Parade over, we lounge about the messroom verandah, where we have tea, coffee, &c., and where brandy and water pegs are drunk by some of the youngsters. Then there is a late breakfast, a morning call or two and billiards. After that comes tiffin, with billiards. Dinner closes the amusements of the day with again billiards, till perhaps midnight. I eschew all the dissipated part of the above amusements and try to keep my head cool for study, which I am prosecuting as hard as one can with the thermometer at 90°. We have had some pretty good amateur theatricals, which were exciting as long as they lasted, but

life in the plains in the hot weather is very trying unless you
have some staff or other appointment in which the work is
congenial to your temperament. After passing as interpreter I shall try for an appointment on the Punjaub frontier
in one of the irregular corps, and then I shall probably see
some service."

Hampton Templemore might well complain of the heat of
Bengal, and to those who have not been in India a sketch of
a day in the hot weather may not be uninteresting. Please
then, kind reader, to fancy that you are our guest at our
home in the district of Tirhoot, some 400 miles to the north
west of Calcutta, and that you are waking out of an apology
for sleep, the last scene of some troubled dream having just
faded away. You find on collecting your thoughts that the
punkah has stopped and that you are as wet as if you had
been in a vapour bath. As a last resource, you languidly
leave your couch, and try if the air in the open verandah will
revive your fevered body. Alas, vain hope!

This is to be one of those days which remind the exiled
European of the heavy price he is paying for the *now* very
questionable pleasure of having a shake at the Pagoda tree,
and it is one of those which draws on his precious stock of
vitality, the exhaustion of which leaves him an easy prey to
the numerous tropical diseases which so insiduously creep on
their victims.

Whew, *it is hot!* There is a portentous stillness in the
air. *Now* a bright scorching arrow of light is thrown on

13

those light fleecy morning clouds which hover over the horizon, and presto! they are gone. A few seconds more and
old Sol surges into sight, a huge, quivering, red-hot ball.

A long succession of rainless months has parched up the soil,
and in the low-lands left it gaping in large ragged cracks,
while on the higher sandy plains the stunted grass is yellow
and to all appearance dead. All agriculture is put a stop to,
for the plough, where it can be urged through the soil,
brings up only brick-like clods. The rivers trickle gently
over the frequent shoals, stagnate in slimy pools, or disappear
altogether. The cattle wander about dejectedly, and in desperation browse on the sapless foliage of the jungle plum, or
rearing on end, pluck the leaves off the trees in the different
groves. Nor, where they slyly can, do they despise a pull at
the old straw thatch of their master's dwelling.

All nature pants for water!!

The hardy native, who generally seems to get cooler as the
white man gets hotter, has now to give in, and fans himself
as he walks along, or keeps his bathing cloth wetted so that
he may swab himself at intervals.

If you attempt to take a ride, your horse is bathed in
sweat, although only moving at a walk, while he is
nearly maddened by the attacks of the large gad-fly, which
brings blood each time it rests on its victim, and whose
high carnival is at this season. If you wish a sensation
gallop, turn your steed towards his stable, and tell him to
go. A bound, a kick, and he rushes like a mad thing to the

welcome shelter. As the sun rises higher, a lurid haze obscures the horizon, which on the flat plains of Bengal is often visible, without a break, from two or three points of the compass. Stand out now, and if you have good strong eyes look at the wonderful mirage. The trees seem to dance high in the air, and yonder herd of diminutive Bengalee oxen are magnified into elephantine proportions. Patiently these stand with lowered heads till it pleases the little naked urchin in charge, who is burnt to the blackness of a cinder, to take them to the nearest water, or to the welcome shelter of some neighbouring grove, the charms of whose shade can now be thoroughly appreciated.

No wonder it is a religious duty in such a land as this to plant the leafy, evergreen mangoe and majestic banian, for without them the country would almost be untenable and impassable to the weary traveller, to whom they are parlour and bedroom and kitchen and all.

Would you wish to examine more closely a Hindoo grove ? Come then, notwithstanding the unpropitious day, don your pith helmet, call the Bearer to unfold the great gaudily painted wax cloth umbrella, while we step across our garden, which, as you see, nearly joins that forest of leafy patriarchs. Ten acres at the least have been planted in lines at distances of about twenty feet between each tree. This would appear to be too close were we not to consider that shade is the great object sought after, and not the fruit, which, however, is borne in great quantities every second year by the mangoe tree.

Not a blade of grass grows under the thick mass of foliage overhead, and we can pace up and down without in the least soiling our thin Indian shoes.

Look at these trunks! Most of them from twelve to fifteen feet in circumference, spreading at ten or twelve feet from the ground into a hundred branches, and bushing out into a magnificent screen of evergreen leaves, the topmost of which is fifty feet from the ground. Try his best, the sun can only here and there dart down an arrow of light, piercing on its way some monster cobweb which shines and quivers in the bright red ray.

No fear of sunstroke here, but it is stiflingly hot. A few minutes more is all we ask you to remain in the oven-like spot, while we watch quietly the little grey squirrel peering slyly down at us, and the green-scaled tree-lizard, who, tongue protruding, pantingly watches for that unwary fly.

Move not! but listen to the rustling midst yon clump of bamboos which fringes the grove. It is the dhamin snake* gliding through the dried up leaves. How listless he seems. He is perfectly harmless, except to birds, rats, and other vermin, so there is no danger in throwing this clod at him, though he looks so formidable and is some nine feet long. *Now*, see how he can travel; head thrown proudly up, and keen black eye glistening in anger at his haunts being invaded! A few leaps and twistings and he is gone, scattering

---

* One of the Boa Constrictor species. The natives fancy that it sucks their milch kine.

in dismay that family of mina birds, who were not at all aware of the proximity of their ancient enemy.

If we were to dig up this hole we should probably find that it contained a jackal, or a pair of them, and with a good terrier or two there would be fine sport for those who like such amusements.

And now back with hasty steps to the house, and call with parched mouth for a glass of sherbet and the punkah. The water for your bath is actually tepid, but bathe you must, and then to dress, an operation of no small trouble and vexation, for no sooner are you out of your bath than the perspiration pours in streams over you, and although the punkah is taking the most vigorous bounds through the air, you cannot keep cool. If you are of Falstaffian proportions, you will spoil at least one clean shirt before you can make your entrée into the breakfast room. Our poor wife comes in dressed in the thinnest of muslins, and imploringly asks us to *speak* to that punkah cooly. He, poor wretch, is pulling manfully, but even *he* is hot, and the perspiration trickles down his face and settles in a drop at the point of his nose. The poor lady's hair is actually sticking to her forehead, and as to the children, one of them, who has just come into the room with only one cotton garment on, has incrustations of salt on its little neck and shoulders, which sparkle like tiny brilliants when she crosses any bright ray of light, while the baby, poor thing, is as red as a lobster from that eruption called in India prickly heat. Nobody can eat anything, and it is unanimously agreed that

if *this* lasts we shall all melt away. We, who are weather-
wise, predict a storm very shortly, and if it does come it will
be a severe one.   It is now two p.m.   The thermometer marks
95 degrees, but this does not really show how hot it is, for the
effect on the human body depends greatly on the presence or
absence of wind.

It is no use to try and remain dressed all day, so ladies and
gentlemen retire to their different rooms, and divesting themselves of boots and dresses, throw themselves under the punkah. We have looked out once or twice on the road which
runs past the house, but no one is mad enough to travel at this
hour.   The birds are silent, our favorite dog has laid himself
in a wet dark corner of our bath room, and we almost feel inclined to follow his example. Were this state of things to continue, Europeans could not live beyond a few days, but
luckily it is not so.   In the North West provinces of Bengal
there is generally a strong west wind blowing, which, acting
on wetted tatties (or screens), renders life bearable, and in
lower Bengal, such a day as we attempt to describe generally
ushers in a tremendous storm of wind and rain, which cools
the air for a week.

It is strange that the several earthquakes which we have experienced in our twenty years' sojourn in India, all happened on awfully hot, still days, and in the deep silence it
is singularly mournful to hear the peculiar wail which the
village women make, when the first shock warns them of the
advent of their mysterious visitor.

On looking out at about 4 p.m. we make sure that, from the appearance of the sky, we are to have one of those terrific gales called in Bengal "Nor-westers." A long succession of rice land lies to the north of the house, then a river, and again on the other side of that, to the horizon, comes a treeless plain. We can therefore plainly see the very first brewing of the storm. There is at the commencement only a thin smoky-looking line of vapour, which, however, gradually becomes denser and denser, till its outlines become black and defined against the sky. Gradually it creeps upwards and hides the sun, and soon it is time to bolt and bar doors and windows, and to see that all fires near thatched house are put out, for it will blow in a way that will astonish any one but an " old hand." The cattle herds know what is coming, and scream to their half-starved charges to try and entice a gallop out of them. There is the shrill call of our old elephant, "Anar Kullee." She knows that there are hailstones as big as eggs in yon black cloud, and screams to be taken under shelter of the nearest thicket of trees, for if elephants are maddened by one thing more than another it is by hailstones.

Our khansamah, or butler, comes in and anxiously inquires what is to be done with the dinner? " Let it wait, Sahadut Khan, till the storm is over, for will not the dust, and then the constant thunder and lightning, make any dinner unpleasant ?" "True my lord. I go to cover everything over till the storm has passed."

All this time there is not a breath to shake the tiniest leaf

on that tall peepul tree, and the mind feels oppressed by the
deadly stillness. The lively, never-tiring, thieving Indian
crow, feels the solemnity of the occasion, and has retired with
his mates to the nearest thicket.

Now a small column of dust comes twisting and twirling
down the road, and we know that the play is going to commence. All still again, and we watch with bated breath for
the first crash. Ah! we were nearly blinded by that flash,
and the old house rings again with the peal which follows
without the interval of a second. A puff of hot air, a rushing
sound, and you are nearly blown away by the cold north wind
which tells of rain and the icy hailstone. Now the hurricane
howls through the nearest groves and against the three-feet-
thick walls of our old-fashioned mansion, almost drowning
the noise of the rolling thunder. It is nearly pitch dark, and
all in the house sit quietly watching the progress of the
storm.

The thermometer will go down twenty degrees within the
next hour, and wise is the man who cases himself in flannel at
once. The house bravely stands the storm, but we have
doubts as to our stable, and think anxiously of our favorite
horses, who are doubtless trembling and starting at every
fresh roar of the wind, or flash of the bright thunder-bolt.
At the crisis of the storm the lightning conductor has been
struck three or four times, and has rattled in its fastenings
as if it would come down.

After half an hour of the most tremendous hurly burly we

know by the rolling sound of the thunder that the worst is over, and we begin to congratulate ourselves on the change there will be in a day or two, when, as if by magic, the grass will be green and the fields alive with the quickly pacing husbandmen, anxious to get in an early crop.

At last it is fairly over. Open doors and windows, and let in the deliciously cool breeze which will dispel all gloomy thoughts, and make us look on life with brighter eyes.

Our rain guage says we have had five inches in this one shower. The ditches are running like sluices, and there are three or four inches of water over our lawn, or compound, as we call it. This is the time for the village boys and the servants to secure a feast of fish. The whole place is alive with them, and men and boys are stumbling over one another in the most amusing manner in their anxiety to secure a basketful. Some of them must have come down with the rain, or how could they be in yonder isolated pool; but the majority have struggled up from the lake at the back of the house, and are making the best of their way to their spawning grounds in the low rice lands which spread for miles in front of us. In an hour or two after the rain, the air resounds with the croaking of countless legions of frogs, full-grown monsters, yellow as saffron, who will line every ditch and tank for miles round. We shall see them to-morrow, in our morning drive, in one continuous string for ten or fifteen miles, and yet if there is no more rain and the pools dry up again, they disappear as suddenly as they came. They must of course bury themselves in the soft mud, and lie hid till the rains set in in earnest.

And thus our hot day ends. The storm we have chronicled is the harbinger of the rains, and for this year our fears of being parboiled are over. It will be damp and dreary enough sometimes, but it will generally be cool. Let us then at last sit down to the long delayed dinner, with real appetite. The wine is beautifully cooled in the hailstones, a store of which has been collected by the servants. There will be no punkah required, and the insects which are the general accompaniment of a hot weather dinner, are all blown away.

And now, kind reader, we will take up the thread of our story, hoping that it may never be your lot to encounter even half the annoyances which are sure to accompany a hot day in Bengal.

CHAPTER XI.

A PICNIC IN THE HIMALAYAHS.

AMONG the two or three hundred families, living for the season at Mussooree, Mrs. Templemore and Laura had selected one with whom they were particularly intimate, the Branscombes.

The head of the family was a civilian of the same year as George Templemore, and remembered him well at College; during their sojourn in India, however, they had never met, having been appointed to widely separated districts. Mrs. Branscombe and his only daughter Jane were with him, the remainder of his children being in Europe. Jane was a thoughtful, sensible girl, and being engaged, like our heroine, to a young man without any great position, but whom she sincerely loved, it was highly natural that their confidences should be unbounded.

"You will see my James," she said to Laura, "when the rainy season is over, he will then get a month's leave, and I hope, indeed I am sure, when you know him, you will like him almost as much as I do."

Laura sighed, and wished that Conrad had not been so far away, but she was too unselfish not to sympathise with her friend in her prospective pleasures, and listened untiringly to all her schemes for the future.

One morning in the middle of October, Jane Branscombe came running into the "Oaks" in a breathless state of joyous excitement and announced the important fact of the arrival of her James at last. "He is determined to make the most of his trip to the hills, and is full of projects for my enjoyment. One of his schemes is a picnic to the Murray Falls, and I have come to-day to ask your permission, Mrs. Templemore (addressing that lady), to take Laura with us. We are only going to have Maria and Lizzy Jones, and a friend of James', a Mr. Wapshott, who rather admires Maria. We shall make such a capital gipsy party, you must allow Laura to come." Mrs. Templemore laughingly gave her consent, and next day was fixed upon for the expedition.

According to appointment, they all met at Mrs. Branscombe's and concentrated their forces before finally setting off.

James Lockley, Jane's fiancé, was a dashing, good-looking, young cavalry officer, and was in the highest possible spirits at the prospect of a glorious ramble on foot, a pleasure impracticable in the plains.

"The falls ought to be especially beautiful at this time of the year" remarked he to Laura, "for just after the rains the volume of water must be at its highest."

Little did he know that these same rains had made sad

havoc with the roads leading to the falls, nor had he asked the advice of any of the older and more experienced residents of the station.   Hence the difficulties that were encountered ; difficulties long to be remembered by those who experienced them.

The distance from Mussooree to the falls was about six miles, and when the road was in repair, there was no danger or any great trouble in reaching them, though in some places the track was startlingly narrow, and the precipices, over which it hung, were terrible in their unfathomable depth.

To the hillmen (Puharees) these breakneck goat paths of the Himalayahs doubtless represent the most delightful of promenades, but to the natives of a level country, they are replete with horrors, and we have seen a native woman-servant of the plains who was making her first ascent to Mussooree, wrap her face up in her sheet and lie down in her charpoy (native bed) while four sturdy hillmen carried it along on their shoulders.   She fancied that being dashed over one of the horrible chasms, was a matter of certainty, so after a little moaning and wringing of the hands, she laid herself down decently to die, and thus corpse-like safely arrived (much to her astonishment) at her mistress's door.

To those who have never seen anything higher than an English hill or have passed half a lifetime in the flat plains of Bengal, the effect produced on the nerves by the awful vast-ness of the precipices of the Himalayahs is as overpowering as it is painful.   No Englishman ever thoroughly attains the coolness and nonchalance of the puharee, and to follow one of the latter for a day's journey, except on established roads, is simply an impossibility.

Numerous accidents happen every year, but as it is the fashion to ride in the most reckless·manner, the only wonder is that more do not occur. This is owing to the sagacity of the horses (the wildest of which become steady on the hills) and not to the prudence of their riders.

Apropos of accidents, we may here record·some which came under the immediate notice of the writer. A gentleman was strolling along the lower road at Landour, accompanied by a favorite dog, which in its gambols ran between his legs, and tripped him over. He fell slightly to one side, and went headlong down some seven hundred feet. The place was not a sheer precipice, but he could not recover himself, and rolled with ever increasing impetus, till he reached the bottom a corpse.

In another instance a lady and gentleman were riding up a narrow bye path leading from the main road to the top of the Camel's back, a hill so named from its shape. Their ponies began to fight, rearing and kicking furiously. In the melée horses and riders broke through the slight side paling and rolled down the steep, which was intersected by the main road at the depth of some two hundred feet, the precipice continuing on the other side of it. In consequence of their being entangled with their horses, nothing but certain death seemed to await them, and yet both were saved in the most miraculous manner. The lady was stopped after rolling clear of her horse by a projecting rock, and the stump of a tree caught her companion in like manner. Their ponies met with a terrible fate, for after reaching the main road their impetus carried them across it, and after breaking the solid rail which was put up for public protection, they were launched over the terrific abyss, and never more seen.

Another poor animal met a similar fate in the following manner :—His master was enjoying himself at one of the evening parties of the season, the horses of the guests being all clustered together on the few feet of level ground surrounding the house. Beneath this was a fall of some hundred feet. The groom after waiting patiently for many an hour, squatted down, native like, with the unfortunate Arab's head rope in his hand, and fell fast asleep. He probably dreamt of his home in the far off sunny south, and forgot the terribly dangerous spot he was on. Suddenly he hears his master's voice, " Get up sleeper, get up." The poor wretch awakes, is flustered, and spasmodically jerks the rope ; now when a horse's head is jerked, he is certain to back instead of advancing, and the rule held good on this occasion ; after a frantic. effort to recover himself, over he went, the very saddle being torn to ribands before his mutilated carcase reached the bottom.

We think our readers will say—enough of such horrors, we therefore return willingly to our picnic.

None of the party knew much of the hills, and the thoughts

of having any dangerous adventures never occurred to the gentlemen, or of course they would have declined taking helpless girls on such an excursion. The Murray falls were one of the lions of the neighbourhood, and that was all they knew about them.

They had with them some twenty Jampanees, or hill porters, who took the ladies as far as practicable in their chairs, the spare men carrying conveyances called Dandees (like hammocks slung on poles) for their use should they tire of walking, the paths being, we may observe, much too narrow for the ordinary Jampan, or chair, used in the hills.

The road at first was quite an ambitious one, being six or eight feet wide, and winding gradually down to a romantic dell, still in sight of the houses of Landour, through which a sparkling stream bustled and bounded along. In Switzerland or Scotland this would have turned the wheel of some quaint old mill, passed by the rose scented garden of some many gabled chalet, or rippled through some picturesquely sited Alpine village, laving the feet of village maid, as she crossed its mimic ford in charge of her flocks. Here, alas, the only substitutes for these poetic accessories was a party of native washermen, bare-legged, bare-armed, and bare-headed, who with many a groan and hiss (ostler fashion) switched high in air, and brought down with sounding thump on boards placed at their feet, long twisted rolls of linen, which once represented shapely garments. Little recked they of crystal stream or clear blue sky, and as long as master's duck pantaloons did not lose too many buttons, or mistress' muslin dress was not in strips, the pretty burnie might run on for ever, without producing any other reflection than, that it was very good washing water, and yielded fourteen shillings a month to each miserable utilitarian.

After leaving this spot, the track at once assumed most shrivelled proportions, here slippery from the dripping of tiny springs which trickled down the mountain side, or there shrinking close to the wall of rock, from whose sides it had been blasted, and round whose giant form it wound zone-like.

Here for the first time some slight misgivings crossed the gentlemen's minds as to their prudence in coming on such a journey without some previous reconnaissance, especially as their fair convoy every now and then uttered little exclamations as they crossed some extraordinarily narrow place.

It was, of course, very pleasant for Mr. Wapshott to hand Maria Jones round projecting angles, which hung like cornices over the oft-recurring precipices, and as long as there was a margin of say two or three feet, it was quite delicious to feel the pressure of her plump little hand as she clung to him for aid, but when there was no margin at all, and one slip sent you literally to nobody knows where, flirting was out of the question. Not only did the path grow narrower, but on the scarped side of it, brambles threw down their cunningly suspended creepers, so that to avoid having their hats torn off or eyes scratched out, it was necessary to keep as close to the precipice as their nerves would allow ; seeing moreover

14

that, on the average, there were only some three feet in width
to walk on, there was not much room for eccentricities of gait.
Crinoline was happily unknown in those days, so by dint of
pinning their dresses in as small a compass as possible, the
ladies managed to get on pretty well, and especially Jane
Branscombe, who, with her James, had lightly tripped some
hundred yards ahead of the rest of the party.

Neither of the Misses Jones, who were from Calcutta, had,
till their arrival at Mussooree, ever seen anything higher than a
molehill, and were terribly bad walkers; but the spirit they displayed on this occasion, deserved the highest commendation.

As the dangers of the road increased, all the little airs and
graces of young ladyhood had to be summarily discarded, and
Maria Jones having stumbled in the most dangerous manner
half a dozen times, Mr. Wapshott tied her shawl baby fashion
in a knot at her back, and held her up by the same at every
one of the bad places. All, of course, walked in Indian file,
and Lizzie Jones and Laura being light and active, managed
almost to keep up with Jane Branscombe, who, with the
assistance of her lover, seemed to flit over places which were
enough to make one shudder. Mr. Wapshott, who weighed
about sixteen stone, and who had long ago given over the
idea of flitting over anything, several times contemplated a
retrograde movement, but the others had advanced beyond
shouting distance; and Maria Jones, his special charge, seemed
to be determined to follow them or die.

Under these circumstances, it was impossible for him to

suggest a more prudent course, so on they struggled with desperate resolution.

At last they came to a place which made their past difficulties appear mere child's play, and in a moment one life was terribly imperilled.

The path had originally overhung a ravine or cleft in the hill side, but was now washed away, they were therefore forced to descend into it, and regain the track by climbing up the opposite side. On the left was a precipice of unknown depth, sheer from the side of which the descent commenced. One of the hillmen stood on the brink of the chasm, another stationed himself a few feet lower down the ravine, and with their aid Mr. Wapshott handed their fair companions one after the other down to James Lockley, who stood on comparatively level ground.

Poor dear Dudu-like Maria, who was the last to descend, did not fare so well as the others. Her feet and ankles seemed to have arrived at a nearly imbecile state.

" A good hold of my hand," said Mr. Wapshott, " now plant your feet firmly above that root, your other hand to the Jampanee, one step, two, three, the next man will have you, and you will be safe." This calculation was a little too rapid however, for without taking time, she, with a small scream, plumped right down on the first hillman, and cut his feet away from under him. He had only to fall backwards, and he was gone for ever, but with native coolness he clutched more firmly the long tuft of grass, with which he had steadied himself from the beginning, and by its aid lightly swung himself back again to his place. The second Jampanee caught Maria before she had gained any great impetus from her fall, and Mr. Wapshott with one hand leaning over, seized her shawl. "Thank God you are safe," gasped he.

She was too frightened to speak then, but she thanked him so sweetly afterwards—of which more anon. The man who had the narrow escape seemed to think nothing of it, and at once smilingly offered his services down the rest of the descent.

After this exciting incident the road was for two or three miles comparatively good, and all recovered their spirits and gaiety, which were, however, soon damped, by their coming to a most appalling place, which we shall try to describe. The portion of the hill out of which the path had been scarped, was composed of a loose mass of shale and pebbles, the artificial supports of which having given way for about fifty feet, the road had slipped, till it formed the same angle as the débris above and below it. The whole was in such an unstable condition, that a stick thrust into it, at once formed a little rivulet of pebbles. About thirty feet below where the road had been, this treacherous slope suddenly stopped, and the usual unfathomable precipice began. Any one, therefore, missing his footing and being unable to recover himself before he reached the chasm was lost beyond recall.

When the rest of the party reached this spot they found Jane Branscombe and her companion holding an animated discussion with the hillmen. She had urged her lover not to return, and the

Jampances had already commenced to make a path, by creeping across the crumbling face of the hill, and patting down with their hands the pebbles in front of them, but even they with their monkey-like feet and slight bodies made deep holes wherever they rested; what then would happen when the heavy-booted Englishmen attempted to cross it?

The gentlemen now thought it their duty to interfere, and said, however much they might be laughed at on their return it was wrong to run so much risk without an adequate object, especially as they had a good excuse in being the first travellers on this route since the rains. But words were of no avail, some horrid fascination seemed to exist in the word *on*, and the four girls were determined to accomplish their purpose at all hazards. A chain was formed, by a dozen hillmen holding each other's hands, from one side of the gap to the other. Lockley, who was to show the way, seized the last one's hand firmly, and then all ran lightly across. The ladies then followed, having the further security of some of the long dandee poles held on the precipice side at about the level of their waists. Last of all ponderous John Wapshott ploughed his way to the other side.

It is no wonder that the natives of India consider all Europeans more or less mad, from the, to them inexplicable, vagaries which they indulge in, and here was a case in point. Four girls did, for hardly any object, what to them was a feat involving difficulty and danger, and yet like high spirited Englishwomen they went through it.

A party of men were set to work to plant boulders along the hillside against their return, and as they were near their journey's end, the day beautiful, and the place they had reached romantic beyond description, they sat down for a while to calm their excitement and silently drink in the beauties of the scene.

The spot they had chosen afforded the greatest breadth of level land they had met in their day's walk, and its beauty invited them to lie down and rest luxuriously mid the long silky grass. Above, was a pure cloudless sky, around, mountains upon mountains raised their majestic forms, while the most tremendous precipices in the world frowned on all sides. The air was perfectly still, not a leaf stirred in the thick forests at their feet, no signs of human habitations met the eye, solitude in its grandest and most awe-inspiring form reigned supreme. Giant trees were diminished to the size of mushrooms down in the far off valleys, or were blended into one indistinct mass of green on the higher ranges of hills, which are here about ten thousand feet above the sea level, while shining above them, in all their indescribable grandeur, the silvery peaks of the snowy range towered into the very heavens, the grandest monument of omnipotence that mortal eye can behold.

It was a dreamy, delicious moment—no one spoke. Picturesquely grouped, they reclined in careless ease on that grassy bank, each absorbed in thought.

The girls, with their hair dishevelled and faces flushed

with excitement and exercise, looked different beings to what they had been when they started in the morning, and were, we have no doubt, not a little delighted at the admiration and compliments which the gentlemen could not help bestowing on their determination and rosy faces.

The small eyed, Tartar-visaged Jampanees sunk down in all possible attitudes in a circle round them, making the fair English girls look all the more beautiful by the contrast.

Dear countrywomen who are lost in the crowd in England, would you be appreciated, go to India and you will realize all your dreams.

After a while, Maria Jones took the opportunity, timidly but with heartfelt emotion shown in each trembling accent, of thanking Mr. Wapshott for the aid he had afforded her; and for the only time in his life that really eloquent young bachelor could not say anything appropriate in reply. There is no doubt, however, that that romantic hillside put, as it were, the last nail into the coffin of his single blessedness, and indeed we cannot help saying that he must have been a hardened wretch if he could have withstood the combination of fascinations of that eventful day. Mrs. Wapshott (late M. J.) often jokes him about it now, and says when her daughters grow up she knows an infallible way of bringing all wavering admirers to the point.

At this place the gentlemen, fowling-piece in hand, sauntered into the adjoining valley in the hopes of finding a pheasant or two, or maybe a brace of the beautiful chick-ore partridge of the hills, but they were not successful, and soon returned to their fair companions.

In half an hour the ladies reluctantly rose, and left the rest-inviting spot, for they had still a mile to go. Up and away is the word, and they march along full of curiosity to behold the far-famed falls which had led them over such break-neck places.

The roar of the water was the first intimation of their arrival at their destination, and after some search (for none of the hillmen had been there before) they found that the approach to the falls lay some hundred feet below. It was a mere semblance of a track, scrambling down which, they were soon encompassed by trees. These thickened as they descended, and gradually formed a canopy over them. A little further on they reached the edge of the mountain side, overhanging the falls, and in an instant the wondrous scene burst upon their view.

On all sides the hills had closed in, forming a narrow bottomless abyss, hidden in its lower depths by dense forest —above the same cause bounded the vision. Down this beginningless, endless chasm poured in a solid stream, a hundred feet high, the irresistible mass of water, the distant rumbling of which came back to the ear in fitful cadences.

These falls are not remarkable for their great breadth, but, as we have explained above, no distinct view of the point from which they leap can be obtained, nor can the eye reach the spot where they thunder down into the valley below.

This makes them all the more mysteriously beautiful, and sets the imagination to work to picture the wild crags from which this embryo river springs, and the awful leaps it must take before it finally settles down in its soft bed of sand far away in the level plains.

The sun shone brightly on the dazzling column of water, while our friends were in the deepest shade, the oak and walnut covering them with their thick foliage, while graceful ferns of every size and hue filled every nook and corner.

After silently feasting on the strange beauties of the place, our party chose a grassy spot, and throwing themselves down discussed the good things they had brought with them. The girls amused themselves by making the hillmen bring them the broad green leaves of the walnut, which they wreathed round their riding hats, thus making them sun-proof for the journey home, while their cavaliers lay at lordly ease, and smiled approvingly.

The lengthening shadows at last warned them that they had their difficulties to encounter over again, so bracing up their strength and courage they started, if not so merrily as in the morning, at any rate more determinedly, and with some of the nonchalance of custom.

After walking a mile or two, James Lockley, who led the way, saw, on the other side of the bay formed by the road following the indentation of the hill-side, a herd of tame buffaloes evidently returning to some village in the direction of the falls, but which had been invisible to our travellers.

A hot flush of blood coursed through his veins, when he thought of the possibility of the sulky quadrupeds disputing the path with them, and he at once ordered on some of the most active hillmen to try to turn the animals down one of the less precipitous gullies, near which they had been feeding.

The spot the ladies had arrived at was one in which the road had narrowed to about three feet, and a wall of rock on the left, some twenty feet high, defied all efforts at escalade, while on the right, the thick tangled forest just topped the level of the path.

It was an anxious moment, for Lockley knew that if the buffaloes, which were only half tamed, once became excited, or saw the unwonted dress of Europeans, they would become quite unmanageable.

Preparing for the worst, he and Mr. Wapshott stood in front of the girls, and dropping a ball into each barrel of their guns, stood breathlessly watching the movements of the Puharees. These last quickly reached the flock of buffaloes, and native like, halloed and screamed to make them leave the road, pelting them with no gentle hand with pieces of rock. The huge, sulky brutes, tossed their horns over their backs, and after staring awhile, grunted out a series of signals to one another, and then for the most part dropped one by one, down to the most convenient ledges below where they had been standing.

One cow, however, which had been severely struck on the head by a stone, and was probably thinking of the calf which she had been expecting to join ere long, would not follow the rest, and with a loud bellow thundered along the track. The puharees threw themselves monkey-like among the trees, and one or two braver than the rest who tried to stop the infuriated animal were tossed over the precipice or galloped over by the infuriated monster, who made straight for the place our friends were standing. As the gentlemen heard the bellowing of the fast approaching buffalo, they begged the girls to lie down close to the foot of the rock, and then with clenched teeth and beating hearts knelt down and cocked their guns.

"Don't fire till she is right on us," whispered Lockley, "let us give her the four barrels all at once, and the chances are we will stop her."

A few seconds elapse—the sharp clatter of the heavy hoofs of the buffalo are heard, as she winds round the few projecting angles which separate her from our unfortunate friends—now she comes full upon them, and suddenly falters as she sees the unexpected apparition of two figures in white kneeling before her. It was impossible for her to turn, and with a louder bellow she rushed straight on. As she reached within a few paces, both guns were levelled, and when Lockley whispered " *Now*," she received the four barrels full in the face.

One frantic attempt was made by her to stop, and then

she tried to turn, but it was useless, a little of the path gave way under her feet, and she was launched headlong into the mass of trees, the crushing branches of which told of the depth down which she had fallen.

The poor girls were nearly dead with terror, and it was some minutes before they could be assured that they were safe.

The puharees having after a while returned, they were put into the dandees and carefully carried along.

None of the men had been killed by their fall, but two of them had broken arms, while one had two or three ribs fractured by the ponderous tread of the buffalo as it galloped over him. The poor fellows were carried along on litters extemporised for them by their fellow porters, and in melancholy procession all slowly wended their way homewards.

The dandees are anything but a comfortable or elegant conveyance, the rider having to sit sideways in the hammock-like cloth of which it is formed, and nothing but sheer necessity could possibly tempt any one, who has a sense of the ridiculous, to get into one of them. The pole comes just under the chin of the occupant, and we must say that a more ungraceful seat was never fashioned. Turning some of the projecting portions of the path the ladies' feet sometimes projected over the precipices, and at these places the slightest stumble on the part of the bearers would have been certain death to all.

Tired and worn out by their exertions both mental and bodily, our party were at length glad to find themselves at the place where their horses and chairs awaited them.

Jane Branscombe and James Lockley saw Laura safely home, while Mr. Wapshott accompanied the Misses Jones, who lived at the other end of the station.

After hearing their adventures Mrs. Templemore could not help saying, "Well Laura, you seem determined to make your experiences of India as sensational as possible. I wonder what Conrad will say when he hears of the dangers you have gone through." Laura could not help feeling the imprudence of her conduct, but determined in her own mind to make all amends she could for it by telling her lover the whole truth when they met, and she felt sure that he would speedily pardon her.

The rainy season being fairly over, Mrs. Templemore once more made ready for a long journey. It was now to be diversified by a trip in one of the river steamers from Allahabad which would land them near their destination, Neelapore. Thoughts of meeting those they had loved rendered the leaving the hills a less unpleasant task than it would otherwise have been, and proved the truth of the remark, that persons more than places make home the paradise it is, or at any rate ought to be. The African missionary, with his wife and family has *his* in an old bullock waggon, still it is home. No doubt love of locality is also a strong feeling, but remove all old friends and relations from your boyhood's haunts, and you will then seek in vain for the charm with which you had once invested them through all your long years of foreign wanderings.

Everything was at last ready, and our heroine and her aunt got into their chairs (the ponies having already been sent on) for the last time, and turned their backs on the glorious scenery which they would probably never see again.

Tramp, tramp, the sturdy little hillmen trot down the descent, past mules laden with the produce of the plains, past groups of hill coolies toiling up with their heavy creels, down through the region of the oak, wild pear tree, gigantic rhododendron and pine, till the clump of bamboos waving at the foot of the pass tells them they are in the plains once more. Now they travel in doolies, long things like meat-safes, as far as Meerut, where their old friend the dawk carriage is waiting to take them down to Allahabad.

Four days of the usual routine of such journeys is passed through, and here is Hampton on his pony come out to meet them, having heard of the probable time of their arrival in a letter from their last resting place.

"Good gracious, Laura," he said, "what a stock of rosy colour you have laid in, and aunt, positively you look like her sister."

You see Hampton was learning the ways of the world pretty fast.

"But you, Hampton, how can you have got up such a

moustache," said his sister, "in so short a time, it is alarming, positively."

Hampton laughed cheerily, and, as he passed his
hand over his upper lip, said that "we military men make
everything subservient to discipline, and why not moustache, ahem!" and with this sage remark he put heels to
his pony and cantered off to apprise their friends of his
aunt's arrival.

The steamer started in a couple of days, and now the
comfortless carriage was exchanged for a nice roomy cabin.

Nothing can be more pleasant than a short trip in one of
these river boats during the cold weather. They are
thatched over from stem to stern, and the whole of the deck
in front of the engine is given up for the comfort of the
passengers. Side curtains keep out the glare of the midday
sun, the river air is cool and bracing and the motion is scarcely
perceptible; so with a gentlemanly and liberal captain and
an agreeable party many a happy hour can be passed on
the bosom of old mother Ganges. At the commencement
of the cold weather numbers of officers and their families
go down by this route to Calcutta on their way to England,
and if they have been long up country, the observant and
critical griff may find ample food for reflection and wonder
at the ease with which people can make guys of themselves
and yet be perfectly satisfied. The bonnets and dresses of
the ladies are some five years behind the fashion, and the
faded washed-out look of the wearers, and their silks and

ribbons, would be laughable were it not almost pitiable. The men are generally ten years older in appearance than they are in reality, and rather affect raggedness as to flannel coats and ruggedness as to beard and hair. They are full of hope at the idea of once more visiting boyhood's scenes, and their wives calculate on being able "to manage *so well* on that extra thousand pounds which John has saved out of his pay," but which gigantic sum dwindles down in so short a time that, poor man, he is glad to make his way back as soon as possible to his old quarters, and hugs his Indian pay and allowances closer and more fondly in his arms.

We must now leave our travellers for a while, and enter upon a subject which will influence the remainder of our narrative.

CHAPTER XII.

THE MUTINIES OF 1857.—THE SHERISTADAR AND THE
BANIAN.—A TENTING SCENE.—THE GIPSY GIRL.

ABOUT this time were heard the first faint mutterings of
the storm which was to dash the crazy fabric of British
power in Bengal to the ground, leaving here and there
intact, that portion which was built, not on the mercenary
affections of its Sepoy army, or supposed attachment of the
people, but on the true hearts and stout arms of its handful
of English officers and soldiers.

Numerous accounts have been written of this great tragedy,
the Indian Mutiny. Each member of Government, both in
India and in England, has thought *his* solution of the
question the right one. The diagnosis of the disease, with
its minutest symptoms, have been faithfully recorded, but
there has been no accord in *naming the cause* of the dread
malady. " Greased cartridges," exclaims one, " That cause,
simple as it may appear, was the real one." " The annexation of Oude had something to do with it," whispers
another. " The paucity of European officers in, and lax
discipline of, the Sepoy army," a third very boldly asserts

15

to be the undoubted reason. This great soldier and that
distinguished civilian had often said the native army would
one day be our worst enemies, but did any man in England
or India act as if he saw into the future? Not one.

In India when the plot began to disclose itself, unbelieving
astonishment was the principal feeling in every breast
among the Government employés, and it is not surprising
that in the European portion, the grossest ignorance of the
machinations devised against them should have prevailed;
but how the Eurasians, forming a large part of the uncovenanted* civil service, and who are half natives by blood,
kept in the dark, was more wonderful, and was decidedly
creditable to the powers of combination and reticence possessed by the wily Hindoo or vindictive Mahomedan.

When we affirm that the European servants of Government were in total ignorance of the plot, and when, also,
we say that it was not astonishing they were so, we may
be asked how this could be? Judges, collectors, magistrates, living among the people, did they hear or see nothing?
" No," we answer, "nothing!" But the reason? Because
they were hedged in by their own vanity, by comparative
ignorance of the language or feelings of the people, and by
a mob of lickspittle, cringing, despicable native officials and
private servants, who persuaded each civilian that he was
the only true incarnation of wisdom, while really the rascals

* Uncovenanted is the term used to describe those civil employés
who did not sign a covenant in England.

had their tongues in their cheeks, visibly to their brethren, but hidden from the hood-winked white man. This may appear an exaggerated account of the matter, but it is not so, and no one with only European experience, can come to a just appreciation of the subject.

Suppose some amiable British nobleman were appointed to administer the law in the Feejee Islands, having only a moderate knowledge of the legal language and intricate customs of those fascinating savages, and being assisted through two-thirds of every difficult decision by his head Feejeean assistant (in India the sheristadar). Suppose, moreover, the Feejeeans to be utterly unprincipled, talented to a degree unknown in Europe in the science of lying, forging, and dissimulation; the most accurate judges of character, and therefore able to fool any one to the top of his bent. Suppose them to abhor any one who is a Christian, with whom all social intercourse is forbidden on account of caste. And lastly, suppose these people to be so reticent, so suspicious of motives, that they weigh each question, and then answer it, not according to the truth, but as it suits them, and you have some idea of the chances of utility of the British nobleman to the Feejeean empire, and you have the exact counterpart of the Bengal civilian.

We do not impugn the understanding of the civilians as a body, for they were average Englishmen, but they were helpless in the hands of their officials, who lived upon bribes, and not only so, but bought large landed estates with the

accumulations thereof.　Go into any district in Bengal, and
inquire whose is that fine house? or who is the proprietor
of such a zemindarry, or grand state elephant? or, in fact,
anything strikingly good, and in seven cases out of ten you
will be told it belongs to so-and-so, who (or his father or
grandfather) was a court official in such a district, the salary
of that office being formerly, perhaps, sixty pounds sterling
a year, and now-a-days say two hundred pounds.

We have one more strange fact connected with this subject to explain.　It is that justice was to a certain extent
to be found in the courts (really though not nominally) pre-
sided over by these men.　*They were too wise to kill the goose
by flagrant acts.*　The established routine was thus :—A
bribe was demanded, through their attorneys, at the commencement of each case, graduated to its importance, from
both plaintiff and defendant, and woe be to either who did
not deposit the same with a mutual friend (a banker), or
otherwise guarantee the payment of it when due.　The suit
was then entered on, documents, witnesses, &c., being all
examined in due form.　The native officials soon saw on
which side the right was, and unless it was a great man
against a very little one, or an outrageously large douceur
balanced against a very small one, generally led their
European puppet to decide in favour of the proper party.
Where every witness was false, or only partially truthful,
and nearly every document the same, this was easily
managed.　The settled commission of the attorneys on each

bribe was ten per cent., and the losing party had his money returned to him.

We may here make a few remarks on a subject, the right reading of which will place the position of Englishmen in India in a clearer light to the European reader, and enable him to realize the inner details of life in the East, without knowing which, he is apt to form his opinions on a false standard, viz., that of his own country.

The topic we would discuss is the position held by the natives of India, as the instruments by which every detail of work whether political, mercantile, or domestic is conducted. On the willingness of the latter to undertake such work hinges our possession of that vast empire ; and from the first day of our landing to the present moment, the co-operation of the natives, whether as allies, or as betrayers of their fellow-countrymen and often kinsmen, or as servants, has enabled us to gain the footing which the mere bravery of our handful of English troops, or the intrinsic merit of the governing units could never have accomplished. This willingness to side with the invader we firmly believe to be instinctive, and therefore decreed by an all wise but inscrutable Providence, which has ordained that for a longer or a shorter period the light of western civilization should illumine the scene which the worn out lamp of ancient heathenism has for so many ages, but with gradually decreasing strength, kept in a mysterious and truth destroying gloom.

No doubt the invincible bravery of our race has been as the spirit of our conquest, but the body containing or co-operating with that spirit, each being a mutual necessity to the other, has been the enlistment of the conquered on our side. This is proveable in a few words, and in fact requires no proof to the thinking Indian reader, but to the uninitiated, we may simply and briefly state, that for eight months in the year, the transportation of a regiment of English soldiers one hundred miles from Calcutta without native agency would be an impossibility. Their live stock and bread materials would firstly be gathered together by natives; their very baggage would be placed by natives on carts guided by natives, or in boats manned by them; and even in the case of the river steamers, the crews of which are all native, we do not believe that European seamen, except in a desperate strait, could conduct them beyond a few days' journey. The grand secret being that physical exertion in the sun is certain death to the white man.

Exceptional cases only prove the rule, and no one, we think, will gainsay our assertion.

Seeing that the above is the case, it will be understood at once why there can be no such class as poor whites in India, and why every detail of life is entrusted to the native. There is a race of Eurasians numbering many thousands; but the respectable portion of it is gradually being absorbed by intermarriage with Europeans, and the disreputable portion is beneath the standard of the natives. As we have said above, we believe there is an instinctive attraction to the white man on the part of his darker brethren; but this does not take the form of love or reverence, not in the least, it takes its material form in the worship of rupees, bright glistening rupees, for which " son has sold father, and brother," brother, ever since our rule commenced, and for generations before that event, during the Mogul occupation.

The one trait in the English character which overwhelms the native by its sublimity, in which he excels the Mahomedan conqueror of Hind by a thousand-fold, is his lavish expenditure of rupees.   To the native, the sums which great and small, from the commissioner of a district down to spendthrift Bill Jones, the indigo planter's assistant, throw about with reckless hands have, for the last hundred years, been conception-bewildering, and soul-entrancing.

"Ingreze Ki Nowkree Dhun Ka Ghur."   An Englishman's service is the abode (storehouse) of wealth.

Thus has said the Hindoo for many a long day, but there have been signs (such as the mutiny of 1857), and there are many now, that the higher classes of the native community have had enough of the foreigners' gold; and when this feeling extends to the lower, there will come a crisis in Indian affairs, the end of which it is not difficult to foresee.

In the mean time, there are multitudes who are slaves of the ring, (of rupees,) and we shall try to show how they behave under its magic influence.

Before, however, lifting our drop scene or introducing

our actors, we must for the second time ask our English reader to accept another great fact in connection with our tenure of India, which will perhaps surprise him as much as the first we have begged him to believe, it is, that in all the governing or official classes, about one pure Englishman in a thousand understands the language of the district he may be in, not as well as Charles Matthews does French, but say as well as a Hebrew professor at Oxford or Cambridge understands that ancient language—ninety and nine out of the thousand can speak it correctly, without having the slightest knowledge of its poetry, proverbs, domestic economy, religion, &c.; five hundred of the remainder can make themselves understood in their courts and offices in a more or less anglicised jargon; and the balance vary in efficiency from the man who thinks he can read and write the language, because he can scrawl two lines of a stereotyped order, to him who wanted to know what Gao was (Hindee for cow), and was told that it was Bāil, Ka, Beebee, or the ox's wife.

In every transaction, whether in a court of law or in a merchant's office, there is a private discussion on the merits of the case held by the native subordinates in secret conclave, of which some of the more astute of their masters have a suspicion, but of which the less experienced know nothing.

Let us analyse a law-suit.

The principal actors in this are—

First. A judge or magistrate.

Secondly. The Sheristadar, who is chief clerk, translator general, reader, interpolator (as it may suit him), influencer, legal adviser, and head conspirator.

Thirdly. The Juban bundee nuvees, or deposition-taker, who writes in the language of the particular district the case is laid in. He is seated out of hearing of the judge, and is conspirator No. 2.

Fourthly. Mohurir who does the sheristadar's junior's work. This is conspirator No. 3, and is of a humble type.

Fifthly. Vakeels or Government pleaders.

Sixthly. Mooktars, attorneys for the litigants.

Seventhly. Witnesses. These are generally professional, and paid from sixpence to ten shillings a day. When they are relatives of plaintiff or defendant they are generally the most disreputable members of their families, who sacrifice themselves on the altar of friendship, and are despised by every one belonging to them.

The first step in a suit is of course to submit the papers to the vakeels and mooktars, who decide on the probabilities of success; not basing such decision on its equity or law, but on the plausibility of its fictitious documents, and the amount of gullability of the judge.

This settled, the mooktar steals quietly at night, (perhaps midnight, for the natives are very owls in their habits) to the sheristadar's house. He gently coughs outside the

wall or screen surrounding all eastern dwellings, and in
answer to the challenge of some dependant who is lounging
about, whispers " It is I, Beharee Lull." He walks in, and
knowing the geography of the place, at once makes for the
verandah where he will find the great man's rossyah (cook),
who is always a favorite confidant. To him he states that
he has occasion to see his master, and is referred to confidant No. 2, generally a fifteenth cousin, and hanger-on of
the sheristadar's, whom we will call Mukes Chunder Ray.
This gentleman calls the mooktar into some verandah or
ante-room, and politely offers him a seat on a mat, then
calls for his hookah, and waits patiently for the story.

This is glibly told, and then a long silence ensues, broken
only by the guggle guggle of the hookah. " Well, Moktar-
gee," at last replies confidant No. 2, " yours is a bad case;
you can't expect me to speak to the Ray sahib (supposing the
sheristadar's name to be Ray, say Bisnauth Chunder Ray)
on such a very poor case, *really you can't.*" The mooktar
knows this is only a form, and so does the first speaker, for
the matter of that. " Hum," he says, "there are certainly
difficulties; but we can get over them. The papers will be
in proper form, and the witnesses excellently tutored, and
of course the Ray sahib need not tell the judge that the
succession in that family is well known by the whole country
side to be in such and such a line."

" Hah, it will be rather difficult to hide the facts; for
the judge becomes more and more particular every day."

"Bhala" (all right), replies the mooktar, " my master is rich, and ——" and here he goes through a certain pantomime.

Perhaps he holds up one finger, meaning thereby one hundred rupees.

This only produces a shake of the head.

Two fingers—

Another shake, not quite so energetic.

Then more fingers, according to the magnitude of the case, and when the amount is settled, the jackal retires to consult the lion who dares not commit himself to any one. After a while he returns and says, " You can come and see the Ray sahib."

After polite salutations, the mooktar probably inquires whether his journey (juttra) will be attended with success, and the oracle answers in similarly enigmatical language, " Yes, if the proper rites are performed, of which my cousin will give you particulars, there need be no fear."

At the due time, the sheristadar stares the mooktar in the face, during the course of the mock trial, bullies him well when the opportunity offers, and goes through the whole farce charmingly; while the poor judge patiently wades through the case, and heartily wishes himself thousands of miles away in any country, where he might have one real friend in court to assist him, and where the atmosphere is not so pestiferous as that of a crowded Bengalee cutchery.

If the dignity of the law is thus made a laughing-stock

of, what shall we say of the details of a merchant's office in Calcutta.

Some of the civilians can talk the language of the country, but the English heads of the trading firms do not pretend to even a smattering of it.

Instead of acquiring the necessary knowledge, they have *ordered* their language to be learned, and seeing the fabulous profit accruing therefrom, all native clerkdom has obeyed.

But this does not advance them a step out of the thraldom which every white man is under in India.

If the judge has his sheristadar, the merchant has a familiar spirit quite as potent, a Mephistopheles who lures him to his ruin, fattening like a horse leech on his victim's life blood, who allows him to sell or buy only as he thinks fit, who worms out all his secrets, and tells him none in return; who finds him in cash, and takes all his profits, he has that veritable skeleton in his closet—the Calcutta Banian.

The whole wealth of Bengal is centred in these men; and when we consider that not one Englishmen in ten for the last fifty years has left Calcutta with *great* riches; while thousands of these scoundrels have amassed colossal fortunes, made in the very offices of the men who have remained beggars; it will easily be believed that the whole of the real profits of trade are absorbed by them.

The banian is a kind of private banker, keeping a certain amount of cash available for his master's business. He also guarantees all sales made to natives, being allowed for so doing, interest for his money, and what is called dustooree, which is about 2 per cent. on every transaction. This guarantee system arises from the absurd custom of there being credit allowed to native purchasers, while the European has to pay cash. The banian being really master, when acting as the slave, is enabled to ascertain the *real* invoice prices of English goods, as well as the real account sales of produce shipped home, and having arranged with his colleagues in their secret rendezvous what is to be done, only allows purchasers to appear who have guaranteed him a certain per centage on the purchase or sale, whichever it may be.

If they see a large profit realizable on any goods held by their masters, they secure them, *be namee*, (that is in another name) at perhaps a trifling rise above the invoice cost; and by their influence they never allow a combination of white men against black, while there is a chronic state of exactly the reverse.

A Calcutta merchant has very tritely remarked, " the European competes, the native combines."

This gentleman has told us that he could hardly ever repeat a favorable order from Europe, from the treachery in his office.

He made a large profit once on a certain shipment, and repeated it for some time successfully. Suddenly his profits stopped, and he found that a man in his office on the magnificent pay of twelve shillings per mensem, had shipped against him, and swamped the market. When he came to

England, he accidentally saw in a wholesale dealer's book, orders from his own banian for the very goods he had dealt in for years. If advices from Europe are not favorable, every banian gives the hint in the bazaar, and up country goods are either held in store, some distance from the capital, or if in Calcutta, none are allowed to be visible. If rates of interest are low and goods unsaleable, the cash balance against the merchant is kept at its highest. If that unfortunate suddenly finds some means of employing a large sum profitably, the banian is ahead of him again, and as suddenly discovers that he has to settle accounts with some up-country dealer. Finally, the grand result of the plot is, that the whole trade of Calcutta is in the hands of the natives, and if they could obtain orders direct from English houses, there would not be a white merchant left. Even this they have done, and are doing, and with a few exceptions of men who have had only dealings with the European population, (such as hotel-keepers, jewellers, &c.) or others who have made some stupendously independent speculations, as lately in cotton, we do not know of one man who has come to England for the last twenty years with a large fortune. One gentleman, who will be recognised by Indians under his soubriquet of King David, left Calcutta with some twelve lacs (£120,000), but more than half of this was made in the China trade.

We have had some princely fortunes lately accumulated by indigo-planters; but for many reasons they are independent to a certain extent of native influence, although they too have to submit to a tax of at least a quarter of their profits.

If they take land, their agent stipulates for a certain bribe, but as indigo cannot be eaten by the population, is only used by native dyers to a limited extent, and is only saleable in Calcutta for immediate transport to England, they come off better than the merchant. Another saving clause for this class is that no native landholder will permit another native to grow indigo on his lands, for fear of broken boundaries, or forged sales during occupancy, whereas he allows the honester Englishman to do as he likes during his lease.

To return to the banian, if our feeble voice can give the key-note to one prolonged shout of reprobation of his rascally doings, we shall consider that a great object is attained, and we would conjure the merchants of Calcutta, if they would thrive, to get rid of them and their system. If there are to be banians, let them be as sworn brokers are in England, who are prohibited from dealings in the articles their principals export or import.

To descend from great things to small, we may remark that from the Khansamah (or superintendent of the cuisine) who gives the unfortunate griff goat mutton, and cooks his food with tallow instead of butter, to the syce (or groom) who sleeps in his master's horse's blanket, and steals half his gram (a kind of lentil), there is one unbroken system of plunder, and the knowing and wearied masters come off the best who allow one man to steal as much as he can safely do, and make him their guarantee against the rest of the robber horde. We could fill a book with amusing and instructive tales about Indian domestics, but we must now return to the consideration of the causes of the rebellion of 1857.

Before stating our own idea of the matter, we will examine the theories of others.

First, then, as to the greased cartridge question. We believe that the dread expressed by the natives in reference to these was entirely simulated, and we can give instances in which the same kind of stalking-horse was used to raise the populace against the government. Two or three years before the mutinies, when English salt was first imported into Calcutta, the natives immediately gave out that it was refined with bullock's blood, and, therefore, abominable. Thousands of tons were, in consequence, thrown into the Hooghly as no one would buy a pound of it. We see that the clearances of that very same description of salt in December, 1862, were 86,000 tons. Again, during the mutinies, reports were spread through every bazaar that bullocks' bones were mixed up with the government-made salt in India, and the population for a time pretended to believe this, but after the success of our arms the report died away, and the consumption of the quasi-polluted salt was never for a moment stopped. No Sepoy really believed that the greased cartridges were intended to take away his caste. Accidental pollution does not always involve its loss to the Hindoo, and under certain circumstances the strict observance of its rules is impossible, hence the declaration to pilgrims that at places like Jugurnauth, or the different bathing or sacred places on the Ganges, caste is not to be considered. A wanton infringement of it is, of course, never overlooked, and if greased cartridges had been served out purposely, after protest, then the Sepoy might have rebelled for that reason alone. But as this was not the case, we say the cartridges had nothing to do with it.

The annexation of Oude is next on our list, and, doubtless, this *****of Lord Dalhousie's did precipitate the rebellion, but it was not the chief cause. Our reason for saying this is, that the general disaffection of the native army must have been correctly ascertained before the grandees and great proprietors of Oude would have run the risk of failure and ruin, by bringing on a collision with our native troops, who, even supposing that portion which was enlisted in Oude had mutinied, could, led by our European forces, have crushed the rebellion in the bud. But the rising was general, not in Oude particularly; and the principal focus was Delhi not Lucknow. Hence we say that the annexation precipitated, but did not cause the rebellion.

Paucity of officers and lax discipline are the last causes in our catalogue. The answer to these is that the natives of Bengal and the north-west provinces from whence our army was recruited, were (especially in the case of the Hindoos) a sober, frugal, penurious race, and in these

16

qualities materially differed from British, or, in fact, any
European soldiery. They were recruited from the respectable yeomen or well-to-do village classes. Now, does
the reader see in these component elements of the native
army anything which would lead him to suppose that they
would ever rebel? We think not. In themselves they
were the representatives of *order*, not rebellion. Paucity
of officers and lax discipline might have made them bad
soldiers, but not rebellious subjects.

Let us name some other causes which might make an
army murder its officers and attempt the ███ � its masters.
First, arrears of pay! Such a thing did not exist. Second,
ambition amongst some of the leading native officers! As
a body, the Hindoos are highly conservative, and revere old
families, rank, &c., and not one Sepoy in the whole rebellion
came out as a general leader, or, in fact, would for an
instant have been allowed to do so. The leadership was in-
stantly taken up by men of ancient family and high station,
for instance the king of Delhi and his sons, Nana Sahib, of
Cawnpore, the Nawaub of Futteghur, Koowur Sing, &c.

Let us suppose patriotism as the cause of the rising.
Again we answer no. This feeling is crushed out of the
people by caste. No five men can be patriots together who
have to cook five separate dinners for fear of one polluting
the other.

We have now given every one a hearing, and will state
our own idea of the case.

The real cause of the mutinies was an intense and general hatred among the native aristocracy, which includes every one of high-caste, to the white man. This was caused by his being the conqueror, by his (sometimes involuntarily so) insulting air of superiority, by jealousy of his bravery, (not of his physical powers, however,) by his radical and levelling method of treating the high-caste native on an equality with the low, (this we have heard them grind their teeth at,) and lastly by an indistinct dread that the time is approaching when Christianity must spread over the land. The annexation of Ou▆▆ ▆▆▆ exactly in the nick of time to consolidate these component parts. A native never bets without a hedge, never does wrong without a previously prepared excuse. They are a logical people ; they like to give a reason ; they gave the cartridges.

They succeeded to admiration in concocting their hell-broth, but its fumes were too potent for the cooks; they spilt it in administering it. Talking plainly, nothing prevented the success of the rebellion, but the want of pluck in its instruments. Intellect against intellect, the native had the best of it. Courage against courage, he was nowhere. But if the hatred was universal, how is it that some stood aloof, some even aided us ? The answer is that the Bengalees were neutral because they are not a fighting race, and had the blessing of a perpetual settlement of their lands at a fabulously low rate. They were certainly neutral, but that was all, and they felt a sullen satisfaction in

looking on at the temporary degradation of their masters.
If the millionaires of Calcutta had come forward as they
ought to have done, there could never have been the panic
which did exist in that city. The lower orders generally
throughout India stood aloof, because the movement was
an aristocratic or high-caste one entirely, by which they
would not benefit, and hence we were supplied with coolies,
boatmen, cartmen, private servants, &c., without whom our
armies could not have moved one inch. If patriotism had
been the moving cause of the rebellion, these would have
gone with their betters; but as we ha██ ███, caste prevented this.

Lastly, some natives befriended our poor naked runaways.
Yes, they did so. Human nature, although rather dis-
torted in the East by Paganism, a low standard of morals,
&c., is still human nature. Men's idiosyncracies differ, and
it is not astonishing that the moderate rebel should have
shown a few feelings of humanity in contradistinction to
the red-hot one who showed none. And now, having nearly
exhausted our arguments, we will return to our story.

Mrs. Templemore and Laura were soon comfortably
settled on board the steamer, which brought them pleasantly,
in about four days, to their destination, Nadanpore. On
the second day they passed the great cotton mart of Mirzapore, and enjoyed the best view obtainable of the ancient
Hindoo city of Benares, steaming slowly under the very
walls of its wondrous conglomeration of temples, palaces,

and ornamental bathing ghauts. The rest of the passage passed without any very striking incidents occurring, and on the fourth evening, as they made fast to the bank at Nadanpore which was the nearest point on the river to their future home, Mr. Templemore was ready to meet them.

After a night's journey by palanquin, they arrived at Neelapore, as day was breaking. They found their house situated on the banks of a lake, which stretched the whole length of the station, and was visible from the drawing-room windows for a mile or two of its winding course. Here and there a thick grove grew down to the water's edge, while the boats of the native fishermen constantly passing and repassing, gave life to the scene. On either side of the mansion extended a tastefully laid out garden, and a flight of steps from the drawing-room verandah led down to the terraced ghaut, at which was lying a gaily painted pleasure boat. Everything exceeded Mrs. Temple-more's expectations, and she soon ceased to regret the beautiful home she had left on the banks of the Hooghly.

In the month of December Conrad Daymer was appointed to an assistant magistracy at Neelapore, and he and Laura were once more together. It was the height of the cold weather, and nature wore her brightest hues.

The usual monotony of life at a moffussil (country) station was broken by visits from the neighbouring planters, races, amateur theatricals, sailing or rowing on the lake, and lastly by spending some weeks in tents, it being a part of each official's duty to make an annual tour through his district. A sketch of this patriarchal mode of life may not be uninteresting, and if we are successful in our picture, our readers will agree with us in thinking that there is a great charm in such luxurious gipseying.

Behold! then. The usual morning fog has just melted away. The sky is blue—a deep Italian blue. The temperature is that of a bright summer's day in England. To the left of the encampment we are about to describe, winds one of the rivers which, rising in the Himalayahs, runs through the district, and yields its tribute to the great Ganges. A short distance down the stream is a native ferry, with its curiously picturesque passengers, grouped here and there, crossing, or waiting to be taken across. High humped bullocks seize the opportunity to take a little rest, and mildly chew the cud, lying down the while beside the quaint-looking carts they have been drawing. Gaily dressed horsemen on fiery little ponies impatiently await the slow movements of the ferrymen. Painted and jewelled native women sit huddled up in that primitive conveyance, the nalkee (something like the palkee), complacently chewing the pungent pawn leaf, or inhaling a few puffs from the cheering hookah. A couple of hideously got up fakeers wander about taking toll from all who are charitably inclined, some giving them a handful of rice, others a pinch of salt or a few cowry shells. They are a poor, frugal race, these Hindoos, and all the finery and colouring that we see is managed for a few shillings. Above the ferry, on the opposite side, is a heavily wooded village, with its bustling bazaar, on the skirts of which a Mussulman mosque shines out in all the glory of a new coat of whitewash. On this side the river the view is limited to the grove, in which the tents are pitched. It is a fine one, perhaps a quarter of a mile long, and nearly as broad, the leaves of the mango tree, of which it is composed, being so thick that the sun can only pierce them here and there with a ray of light.

What a busy scene meets the eye, as we enter its grateful shade!

These three or four holes, cut in the ground, in which are bright charcoal fires, protected from the wind by a few mats, form the kitchen, from which none but an Indian cook could conjure the marvellous dinner he does. Everything appears nice and clean and those frizzling lamb chops give one quite an appetite to look at them, while if we lift this cover, we shall find the most delicious of omelets nestling beneath it. Conveniently close is the servants' tent, in front of which, as you see, the khansmah and khidmutgars are robing themselves for breakfast.

A little further on, knee deep in fresh rice straw, are three or four satin-skinned Arabs, and our two little friends, the ghoonts, which have come all the way down from Mussooree. They are picketted under the trees during the day, but yonder

is the stable tent to shelter them from the night winds and
dew.   On the other side of the stables is the cutchery or
office tent, guarded by a file of Sepoys.   Complainants, de-
fendants, and witnesses are grouped about under the trees in
deep converse with the vakeels (pleaders) and mooktars (at-
tornies) preparatory to the opening of the court.

Now let us turn back again.   Under *the* tree of the grove
is stretched a shamianah or awning of striped white and red
cloth.   On the ground beneath this is spread first a layer of
clean straw which is hidden by a drugget, and above all is a
bright Mirzapore carpet.   In the centre a camp table is laid for
breakfast, round it are three or four easy chairs, and, lastly,—
most charming sight—are seated our two English ladies, dressed
in light and elegant morning robes, one of whom is just pouring
out a cup of fragrant tea, while the other is working and at
intervals watching the curious panorama before her.   Behind
the shamianah is the reception tent, and again in the rear of
that are those for sleeping in.   These last are surrounded by a
wall of cloth (kanauts) eight feet high which hides them from
the public gaze.   The grove is perfectly free from bushwood
or undergrowth of any kind, and is dry and clean throughout.

Mr. Templemore now walks in.   He has been out for an
hour or two shooting and lays his trophies at Laura's feet
to be admired.   There are a brace of black partridges of
beautiful plumage, a fat little grey quail and a small Indian
hare.   The sportsman looks so rosy and so farmerified in
gaiters and velveteen coat that one can hardly believe he

is an old Indian and that in an hour or two he will be transformed into the solemn judge. He is followed by the dawk-wallah or postman, who throws down a bundle of papers, letters, and magazines, which are eagerly opened, especially a little note from Conrad, and examined.

"Here's more of that chapatty business," said Mr. Templemore as he scanned the last Calcutta news, " I wonder what it means, none of my amlah seem to understand it at all, and yet they ought to know." "I see our friend Desmond," he continued, "has got his majority, and his regiment is ordered to Nadanpore. I should not be surprised if he rides over some morning to see us. By the by, what an assistance he would be in our theatricals."

Breakfast over, Mr. Templemore goes to office where he will be engaged till the afternoon. The ladies write letters, work, and gossip till the lengthened shadows warn them to get ready for their evening ride.

Here are their horses, mincing, and tossing their heads behind their smartly dressed grooms, who with silver-handled chowry, or yâks tail, in hand bring up the pets to have their little tid bits of sugar cane. They are called Butterfly and Peacock, one a bright chestnut, the other a very purely-bred flea-bitten gray. Butterfly's characteristic is that he has peculiarly light paces, and the gray holds up his tail so much like a picture-horse, that hence his name. Mr. Templemore rides a larger, heavier animal than either of the others and it is as much as he can do to keep up with the ladies. They ride about exploring here and there, now looking at a ruin, now admiring some curious freak of nature, such as a peepul tree growing round an aged palm, which it has encased in its roots, and will gradually cover over altogether. The palm will not die, however, for many a day, and will year after year wave its feathery frond from out its destroyer's bosom. Now 'tis a fisherman whom they stop to watch, he is throwing the peculiar kewla net of Bengal, unknown in Europe. See, he gathers up a portion in his hand, it looks a mere entangled mass. Whisk! it flies round his head, and lands on the water a fair unwrinkled circle of nine feet in diameter. It is leaded round the edge, and held by a string attached to the centre. Pull this, the weights bring the edges together and lo! a dozen sparkling chulwas and pubtas* are added to the basket swung at his back.

"Who are these?" said Laura to her uncle, as they passed a straggling cavalcade of natives whom even she could see were of a different race to the inhabitants of the district they were in.

He had barely time to answer her question by saying they were gipsies, (nutts, in Hindustanee) when one of the women, a tall, bright-eyed, bold-looking girl ran in front of his horse and, at the risk of being ridden over, held up her baby close to its head. Half whiningly, half impudently, she said, in strange Hindustanee, "for the sake of the nunkee (little one), make your poor slave a present."

* These are two of the commonest species of fish in Bengal.

He was annoyed at her impertinent manner and told her to be off for a shameless one. The girl tripped back to her companions screaming with laughter and jokingly alluded to her having bantered the white man.

A wild, shaggy-bearded, desperate-looking set of ruffians were the men. Their long locks hung down to their waists, or were tied up in huge shapeless masses, bleached into dirty red by exposure to the weather. They reminded one of wolves, they were so gaunt, so sulkily-fierce looking. You could tell their race at a glance. Nothing can hide the true gipsy eye. Once seen in the nutt women of India it can never be forgotten. There is a size, a wild glitter in that dark orb, which is absolutely fascinating. This party, as one of the grooms ascertained, had journeyed all the way from the burning plains of Scinde.

"They call themselves Khuttuks by race, but they are a bad set or I'm mistaken," said the man, shaking his head.

They had numerous donkeys and buffaloes on which they carried their tents made of the sirkee reed sewn together, with their charpoys or beds and other household gear.

Mr. Templemore was astonished to see, also, that they had a number of English dogs with them of all kinds, from the greyhound to the little spaniel, and he wondered much where they could have possessed themselves of these. "They have stolen them, I suspect," he said to his wife, "from the different cantonments they have passed through, and I must tell the police to keep an eye on them, especially as we are in

curious times." "I don't like their looks at all," he muttered, as they rode on. And now the evening fog gently
creeps over village and grove, mingling with the smoke of
the wood fires just now beginning to be lighted to cook the
much-loved evening meal, and presses it down to the ground
nearly choking our party as they ride through some native
hamlet or bazaar.

The snow white heron, tired with his silent, monotonous
day's work, flies lazily home, uttering discordant greetings to
his brethren, whom he hastens to join in yonder tree. The
giant cricket suddenly commences his ear-piercing performance, and almost prevents you hearing what your companion
is saying, his *whir-r-r-r* is so distressingly loud. Everything cries " Homeward !" The lowing herds come straggling down the lanes, crowding and struggling as they press
through some narrow pass, while the thumps showered by
the herd-boys, on their drum-like sides resound through
the still evening air. Darkness comes on very suddenly in
India, our friends must therefore haste or daylight will be gone.

Now Butterfly, now Peacock, pull your fair burdens' arms
nearly off, as you rush home to your suppers, but no jostling,
and no pretending to bite one another, no ! let it be a fair
race, and we will back the Peacock to take his laughing and
flushed rider first to the edge of the grove. Grove did we
say ? that word does not describe it. It is a scene at the
opera ; there are the watchfires and the robbers, and gloomy
caves, and bright bits and vistas in the trees, ending in black

darkness.   There are the captives bound and awaiting their
fate (the court prisoners), and here is the brigand chief's tent.
Well, it is a very comfortable one and his people seem to
know how to spread a dinner table remarkably well.   So
covers off, if you please, khansamah, and the bandit and his
women will dine.

At day-break next morning, as Mr. Templemore was
sipping his early cup of coffee under the shamianah (awning),
and most of the camp followers were still asleep, he was startled by seeing a woman with dishevelled hair and blood-
stained garments rush through the trees, and throw herself
frantically at his feet.

"What in the name of Heaven is the matter?" he said,
leaning over, and trying to raise her, but she only grovelled
the more on the ground, wildly repeating, "Ai ullah, ai ma;
oh ullah, oh mother!"

He thought she must be mad, and made two of his orderlies
raise her up, when to his further astonishment, he recognised
the gipsy girl of the previous evening.

The men gradually soothed her, and in broken, gasping
sentences, she told her tale.

"I am the nutteen (the gipsy girl) your lordship knows.
They married me to the Sirdar (leader) of our gang; you
may have noticed him—the tall gray-haired man.   Of all the
ruffians he is the worst.   He used to beat me.   I bore all
for my child's sake—you saw it, a little thing, soft as a ball
of cotton."

Here she tried to throw herself down again, but was forcibly held up by the men, who sprinkled water over her face, and begged her to continue her story.

"I will," she gasped. "Well, last night, in one of his drunken fits, he took up his hatchet because I had burnt his rice, and (here her voice became almost inaudible from emotion) he killed the nunkee (the little one). I had blood for blood," she whispered. "I stabbed him—once—twice, but he did not die. They seized and tied me down with cords. I bit them through, and flew to your lordship's feet for justice. Send out your police; the whole band are thugs. Break open the legs of their charpoys (camp beds); they are hollow, filled with jewels and money, robbed from road-side traveller or strangled villager. Be quick! The men will scatter when they find me gone. Oh, my child! my child!"

Mrs. Templemore and Laura, hearing the screams and moans of the wretched woman, hastily put on dressing-gowns and came out to ascertain the cause, and after learning the story from her husband, the former made the girl over to her woman-servants to be watched and taken care of.

Mr. Templemore roused the camp, and sending messengers for aid to the nearest police-station, started a party in pursuit of the gipsies.

As the woman had predicted, not a man was found in their tents. The women, much to their pretended surprise, were marched off to the police station, with all their goods and chattels, and on their beds being examined, the legs were found to be filled with all kinds of valuables, among which were jewelled nose-rings, bracelets, and in one, some hundred counterfeit rupees, each coin wrapped up in cotton, to prevent it jingling while being carried along.

After a short pursuit, the party sent by Mr. Templemore came upon the leader, who, weak from the wounds he had received from his wife, could not keep up with his comrades, and had been deserted by them. He was secured, and from inquiries made of the villagers round about, it was found that the band had made for some heavy grass cover, which extended along the banks of the river. A few of them were caught, after four days' search, in a wretched plight from want of food, and some managed to escape into the territory of Jung Buhadur, of Nepal, where they were safe.

In due course of time those who had been captured were tried. The leader was condemned to death for the murder of his child, and one of the gang having turned Queen's evidence, the others were all transported for life.

The unfortunate gipsy girl sank into a state of low melancholy, and was looked on as quite harmless. One day, however, her keepers missed her, and not for a week did they receive any tidings of her fate. Her body was at last washed ashore some miles below the station she had been removed to, and it was conjectured that in a fit of despair she had thrown herself into the stream.

CHAPTER XIII.

THE DUEL.—POOR STRUGGLES.—THE AFFAIR AT ARRAH.

As Christmas drew near those residents of Neelapore
who had been living in tents, returned to the station to
feast and be as merry, in as English a manner as circumstances and climate would allow. Ladies read up receipts
for mince pies and plum pudding, while the gentlemen
(much to the horror of the Hindus) paid enthusiastic visits
to the fattening oxen, joints of which were to crown the
festive board.

The weather was serenely bright as it generally is at this
season, and no very heavy clouds, up to this period, having
obscured the political horizon, men saw no reason why they
should not enjoy themselves as much as formerly. Races,
theatricals, cricket, dancing and dinner parties, with rowing
and sailing matches on the lake, all combined to make the
time pass pleasantly. Everybody ran something at the
races and the excitement was, therefore, as general as it was
great. This feeling, however, soon cooled down, when the
owners discovered that untrained horses cannot gallop

without suffering for it, and the number of thick legs and stiff shoulders in the different stables became quite alarming.

Among those who had been invited to join in the gaieties, and were generally the leaders in the sports and amusements, were Major Desmond and a party of officers from Nadanpore. Desmond was looking more haggard and older. The hue of health which he had brought with him from England, had given place to a pallor which made his dark eyes more expressive by the contrast, and it was evident that climate and dissipation were telling upon him fast.

He entered into all the amusements with an apparent abandonment and gaiety, but Laura noticed once or twice that he would suddenly fall into a reverie, with his eyes fixed on vacancy, though the moment before he had been as loud in his merriment as the rest. He had, of course, heard that Laura was engaged, but had not in any way alluded to it, although his conduct made it evident that his smouldering jealousy only awaited an occasion to burst into a flame. Once or twice he nearly provoked a quarrel with Conrad, refusing to row next him in one of the pleasure boats, and at another time contemptuously throwing a cricket ball at his feet, instead of tossing it to him courteously. Conrad was not one to put up with the slightest insult, but the instances we have mentioned were just those kind of impertinences which were hardly worthy of serious notice. He had, however, a presentiment that something more marked would oblige him to call Desmond to account,

17

especially as it was seen by all that the latter often drank to an extent which rendered him incapable of weighing his actions.

On the night of the last ball at the station, as Conrad was walking with Laura after one of the dances, she drew him gently into the verandah and said—

"Do you know, dearest, that I am very much alarmed at the way Major Desmond acts towards you, and for my sake I hope, now that he is going away, you will not allow yourself to be drawn into a quarrel. He seems to be in such a fierce reckless mood, that I believe him capable of any extravagance, and this evening he has been drinking a great deal too much champagne."

"Yes," replied Conrad, "the man is half mad with drink and jealousy, and were it not that I abhor a scene, I would bring him up before he left the room, but two or three of my best friends whom I have spoken to, advise me to keep out of his way. Had we been living at the same station I am afraid nothing earthly could have prevented some open disagreement."

Laura again reiterated her request, and they re-entered the ball room, both looking sad and lost in thought. At the conclusion of the evening Desmond came up to her and stood for a few moments at her side without speaking; then suddenly bending down, he whispered "I have to congratulate you, I believe, Miss Templemore, on your engagement to Mr. Daymer." He paused as if waiting for a reply.

Laura stammered out something unintelligible, and felt as if she must faint. Her face became pale, then flushed, and the room seemed to swim round. Still he waited, and again bending over her, muttered, *may my curse follow him to his dying day ;* and without another word abruptly left the room.

Laura feared to tell any one *then* of what had happened, and was glad to see Conrad approaching to escort her to the carriage and to know that he had been able to avoid a collision with his infuriated rival. " Go home," she whispered, " dear Conrad, if you love me, go home."

Unfortunately he had engaged to play a match of billiards after the ball, which broke up early, he therefore jumped into his buggy and drove to the room, which was a detached building at the other end of the station. On entering he put down his name on the slate, and his friend being already there, they only waited till they could claim the table.

Just as the game in progress was finished Desmond and some of the officers sauntered in, and the former scowling on Conrad, went up to the slate, and not in the clearest accents told the marker he should play next.

The man replied " the table is engaged by Mr. Daymer, sir."

" Oh! Mr. Daymer is always first, is he? He must wait this time. Come along Russel, get your cue and we'll begin."

There was, of course, a murmur through the room, and

several of the men were about to interfere, when Conrad saved
them the trouble by walking up to the table and, placing
his cue upon it, requested Desmond, in as quiet a tone as
he could command, to allow him to begin his game. The
latter, who was in the quarrelsome stage of intoxication,
only answered by placing *his* cue across Conrad's.

This was more than any man of spirit could endure, and
he dashed his hand up so violently that one of the sticks
struck Desmond smartly over the forehead.

As quick as lightning the latter brought his cue down
on Conrad's head, who, however, saved himself by warding
off the blow, and the bystanders at once separated the
combatants. Desmond was taken into another room foaming with passion and declaring that he would have his
rival's life. "He brought it on himself, and I'll shoot him
if I can."

There was a gloomy silence in the billiard room, and
every one foreboded mischief. At last Russel, whom we
have mentioned, walked into the room, and, waiting till
Conrad had finished his game, beckoned him aside and spoke
a few words. They were to the effect that Desmond demanded instant satisfaction, that it was a bright moonlight
night, and that he was waiting near the big mango tree
by the lake. Conrad replied " he shall not have long to wait,"
and, asking his friend to accompany him, they walked away
to the appointed spot. One sickening thought of Laura
and of those dear to him in England crossed his mind ; but

the die was cast; he could not now retreat. He, however, made up his mind what course he should pursue and briefly mentioned his intention to his friend, who quite approved of it.

After the seconds had conversed a little, Conrad's came up to him and said, " Desmond insisted on being put up at twelve paces, but I have arranged it is to be fifteen. He seems almost insane, and if he misses the first shot I shall take care he does not have a second."

They were placed opposite one another, the word was given, but the report of one pistol only sounded through the night air. It was Desmond's, whose ball had pierced Conrad's side. He staggered as he felt the shock, but mustering up all his courage, advanced a pace or two and said—

" You have had your satisfaction I presume, Major Desmond," but to show my utter contempt of such worth-lessness as yours, I take mine differently—*thus ;*" and firing his pistol in the air, sank into his second's arms. The medical man present at once examined his wound, and found that, although bleeding profusely, it was only superficial, the ball having glided over the ribs. After bandaging it up, he was lifted into his buggy and driven home.

Desmond seemed unsatisfied at the result of the meeting, and as he left the ground muttered something about future revenge.

At day-break he took his departure from Neelapore, with hatred and jealousy still gnawing at his heart, mingled with the certain knowledge that he had estranged himself from the society of the Templemores for ever.

Mr. Templemore, who had been awakened by the station doctor, accompanied that gentleman to Conrad's bed-side, and was at first much alarmed at his appearance, but after being assured by both medical men, that, humanly speaking, a fortnight would see him convalescent, and in compliance with Conrad's entreaties, he hurried home to relieve the anxiety of his wife and Laura, who were awaiting his arrival in a state of great agitation, not knowing exactly what had happened. The latter had dropped some hints to her aunt as to Desmond's conduct during the ball, and they were therefore not so much surprised as they might otherwise have been at Mr. Templemore's account of the affair, and both felt relieved and thankful that matters were no worse.

In a few days, when all symptoms of fever had passed away, the two ladies were constant in their visits to Conrad's bungalow, and Laura was now enabled to return some of the fond care and attention which she had received from her lover in Calcutta. The cruel attempt which had been made to sever them only increased their devotion, and, secure in each other's affections, they looked forward to the future with the hopeful feelings of youth, and the consciousness of the purest and most disinterested love.

In a month's time Conrad was again at his official post, and was nearly as strong as ever. He and the other residents of the station now began to have their suspicions that the flying rumours of the past three months had something more in them than the every-day exaggerations so loved by the gossiping natives. An officer at Barrackpore (near Calcutta) had been cut down by one of his men, who had been aided and abetted by his brethren in doing so. Luckily the native regiments there and at Berhampore (60 miles off) were immediately disarmed. If these men could have stuck to their original role, which was a simulation of loyalty till all the European troops were ordered away from Calcutta, that city would have been the scene of a terrible conflict. The bravado, however, of one drunken scoundrel, spoilt the plot.

Hardly had this news grown stale when rumours came down of rebellion at Meerut, then at Lucknow, and as the sun became more and more unbearable to the white man, so each station rose.

We will not discuss the old question of incapacity here or infatuation there; somehow or other we blundered through the ordeal, and doubtless by the fiat of Providence, working through the instrumentality of the British army, the empire was saved. But what if the Sikhs had joined the mutineers? or the Chinese troops had not (by chance) been available? or the lower orders of India had struck

work ? Without a question the country would have been
lost to England.

One morning as Mr. Templemore and his family were
sitting at breakfast, the post came in, and after reading, or
rather glancing at, the numerous items of news, all containing more or less gloomy tidings, he suddenly started, and
said to his wife, " What do you think, my dear, there has
been a terrible *esclandre* at Nadanpore, and Major Desmond is the hero of it."

Both Mrs. Templemore and Laura eagerly asked what it
was.

" I will read you an extract," he replied : " ' There has been
a terrible exposure here. A letter has been received by the
Colonel of Desmond's regiment, written by a person in
England, who claims to be the wife of the latter. [Here
both ladies uttered an exclamation.] She says that having
heard a report that he was about to marry the niece of
some civilian in India, she could not allow an innocent
girl to be sacrificed, when the disclosure of her existence
would prevent such a crime. That from her husband's
cruel conduct and dissipation of her fortune by gambling,
she had, some ten years before, taken refuge in flight, sup-
porting herself by different methods, but latterly by taking
the situation of nursery governess with a Russian family in
Paris. That with the connivance and assistance of her
friends she had eluded all pursuit, and had even advertised
her death in the papers, and that so far he was blameless.

She concluded by saying that every necessary proof of her assertions was ready, but that Major Desmond would hardly dare to deny the truth of her story. The Colonel immediately showed Desmond the letter, and was shocked to find that he could give no denial to the facts, though he solemnly asserted that he thought his wife was dead. As the regiment was ordered on active service, Desmond could not leave it, but it was supposed he would sell out at the earliest opportunity.' "

" What a terrible rascal the fellow seems to be," said Mr. Templemore. " I suspect, my dear," addressing his wife, "that you will not again in a hurry be fascinated by a polished exterior only, and you may thank your stars, that the civilian's niece was not made the victim of such a villain." Mrs. Templemore seemed to feel her husband's remark acutely, and with tearful eyes, holding out her hand to Laura, said, "You have forgiven me long ago, Laura, have you not?" " Yes," said the latter, kissing her tenderly, "I have, and if this sad experience should strengthen your regard for me, I shall almost remember the subject with pleasure instead of with terror and disgust."

After opening some other letters, Mr. Templemore looked up with a curious expression on his face, and exclaimed, " Here is some extraordinary news from Khosamudpore. From what my friend Douglas writes, poor Montmorency Struggles must have been badly used. He says, 'we were

petrified last night by the apparition of the Commissioner
of Khosamudpore riding into our compound, dressed very
badly as a native, on a terribly thin and broken down pony.
It seems that after the native troops at the station mutinied,
he was by some accident prevented joining the other
fugitives, and was laid hold of by his amlah (native officials)
to whom he had been so kind, and made to suffer great
indignities. They actually bound his hands, and sat in
judgment over him in his own court. They addressed him
as the motha soor, (fat pig), as the churbey dar (the fat
one) and wished to know when he thought they would
become Christians. Some of the Mahomedans proposed to
make him join their sect, while others suggested hanging.
At last they abandoned these ideas, and in place of them
adopted what they doubtless thought a good joke. They
made poor old Struggles put on a Khidmutgar's drawers
and skull cap, shaved off one of his whiskers, and giving
him an old greasy sheet to throw over his body, mounted
him on the most wretched tatoo they could find in the
place, and pelted him with clods, till he made it gallop.
Poor man, he was not able to get out of bed for two days
after he reached this, he was so stiff and sore. You
remember Struggles always loved the natives so much.
Well, he *does* love them now. He is an altered man. He
has got hold of a tremendous cavalry sabre, which he is
constantly sharpening, and swears that he will have his
revenge. The first party of troops that goes to Khosamud-

poor will have him with them, and if he can only catch his
sheristadar (head native assistant), I firmly believe he will
eat him or a portion of him at least.' "

"A nice state of things, is it not?" continued Mr.
Templemore. "The world seems to be turning upside
down altogether, when these cringing smooth-tongued,
sententious natives can mix up jocularity with their
cruelty. I have long had my suspicions that we did not
know them thoroughly, and it appears I was right."

After a pause he again addressed his wife, this time with
a grave aspect, while the care-lines in his face seemed to
deepen as he spoke—"There is worse and worse news from
all the up-country stations above Benares, where there has
been a fearful conflict, and the next place to enter the
flames will, I am afraid, be Allahabad.

Mr. Templemore leant his head on his hands, and remained
buried in thought, while the ladies were struck dumb by
the evil tidings they had heard, and, asby pale, sat motionless in mute despair.

Who shall describe the feelings of the dwellers in Bengal
during that dark period of trial? They felt that they were
such a handful among the myriads of natives, who had shown
so little mercy to those who had fallen into their power. The
horizon looked black indeed. Men's hearts sank at the con-
templation of the awful odds arrayed against them, and for
a time were chilled by hopeless despair. Then would come
that glorious inspiration, which is the birth-right of each

true-born Englishman, that feeling which saved India, and has led them on to heroic deeds from their remotest history, which the degraded Asiatic has not in his servile breast, and which, in the hour of his direst need, cries to each free-born man, *Do, and fear not to die!*

" Poor Hampton," sobbed Laura, "I hope his regiment will stand fast; his last letter was full of hope, was it not, uncle?"

He shook his head, and said, " If they secure the fort, there is a chance of things going right, but they have only some seventy old invalid Europeans, and the handful of troops with Neil may not reach in time."

This was the brave Major Neil, of the Madras Fusiliers, who was killed at Lucknow after the most brilliant services. He and he alone saved lower Bengal from at least temporary conquest.

To give a detailed account of the mutinies is not our object. We will, therefore, only relate those circumstances which particularly influenced the welfare of the friends whom we have introduced to our readers.

When Mr. Templemore and the other residents of Neelapore found matters becoming daily more threatening, they determined to send off their families to take shelter in the nearest military station, which was Nadanpore, or to Calcutta, but breaking up their establishments would appear such an equivocal, or rather unequivocal, act of timidity, that it was put off to the last moment. The officials, too, of Neelapore, were placed in a doubly difficult position from having a very

large amount of treasure in hand, which they were afraid to
send away, afraid to keep, and which they dared not abandon
till the last extremity. The troops at the station consisted
of a jail-guard of some two hundred men, a perfect rabble,
only formidable to their masters, and a troop of irregular
cavalry, which had been sent by the commanding officer of
the nearest military station as an extra protection, but which
only proved an extra curse.

Before the end of another week the news became so
alarming that the day was fixed for the ladies' departure.
On that very morning, however, the distressing tidings came
in that there had been a terrible disaster at Nadanpore, and
that the roads were now impassable, being infested by bands
of insurgents, who watched for any stray Europeans like
hungry hawks. When Mr. Templemore communicated these
tidings to his wife and Laura, they clung round him, and
begged him not to distress himself on their account, as they
were prepared to share his fortune, whatever that might be, and
he had at least the satisfaction of knowing that they were
resigned to their fates. Conrad, who had urged their departure long before, now did his best to solace them by various
arguments, all tending to show that as Government assured
every one that the rebellion was only a military *emeute*, it
must speedily be put a stop to on the arrival of reinforcements.

The actual inhabitants of the district round Neelapore
were still perfectly quiet, and no one believed that matters

would proceed to extremities. All eyes were anxiously turned towards Nadanpore as the key to their position, and details of the catastrophe which had occurred there were eagerly looked for, but the irregularity of the post, consequent on the blockade of the roads, prevented the news from reaching for some days. At last one messenger forced his way through and the worst was known. The three native regiments at Nadanpore had mutinied, and by the imbecility of the General commanding had been allowed to slip away, when they might have been attacked and at least prevented doing further mischief. Instead of this they marched in a body to a civil station some twenty-four miles distant, and laid siege to the handful of civilians and others who had fortified, and heroically defended, the post. When it was found that they must be massacred unless assistance were sent, an expedition was organised and despatched for their relief, which resulted in the loss of nearly one-third of the European force stationed at Nadanpore. This was the fruits of the most woeful mismanagement, and as a specimen of how the bravest troops may be sacrificed is worthy of record. The officer sent in command was notoriously unfit for the task, and it was said of him, as the detachment moved out of their quarters, " He was never anything but *too late*; this time the odds are that he is *too soon*. " This was verified to the letter, and retribution followed swiftly on his unwarrantable neglect of the most ordinary precautions to prevent a surprise.

The small force of some three hundred and eighty Europeans

and fifty Sikhs, with ten or fifteen volunteers, started, full of hope, in one of the river steamers, which conveyed them to within twelve miles of their destination. Before, however, they had been many hours in the crowded vessel, they were completely overpowered by the heat, and, half dead with exhaustion, began their long journey in the afternoon. They had no proper meal the whole of that day, and at one of the halts were so completely exhausted that they fell asleep as they sat, and begged to be allowed to take a short rest. No! they were doomed. On their arrival at a thick grove, half a mile from the station they were marching on, the advanced guard of hardy Sikhs passed through, followed by the half asleep, staggering Europeans. Suddenly they were aroused by the deafening report of three vollies from the muskets of at least fifteen hundred men. They were dead beat, trapped, and in the confusion each man shifted for himself. The Captain in command was one of the first who fell. Those who escaped sheltered themselves for the remainder of the night behind the bank of a tank, but at last had to retreat, their relentless pursuers being afraid to close with their worn-out enemy, but taking advantage of every ridge and mound to deliver their shots.

Here the brave Mangles won his Victoria Cross, carrying a wounded comrade three miles on his back. Here also the gallant McDonell gained the same decoration for his generally heroic conduct, but especially for clearing the rudder of the boat (amidst a storm of shot) which conveyed the fugitives across a stream, lying between them and the steamer.

Out of the little band only one hundred returned unhurt, the rest were all killed or wounded, and the reception of the party on their return by the wives and families of the poor men, will not soon be forgotten by those who witnessed their frantic gestures and heard their heart-rending screams, when they were told of the terrible massacre.* One body of Irishwomen went off howling to the General's quarters, and if he had not hidden himself (as it is reported) would have taken summary vengeance on him there and then. Thus ended this calamitous affair. The besieged station was ultimately succoured, in a few days, by a small force of two hundred men, properly led, thus showing what might have been done by the Nadanpore troops.

Let us now see how it fared with Hampton Templemore in these dreadful times. His regiment had been so virtuously indignant at the mere suspicion of disloyalty that the Colonel was prepared to defend them from all traducers and wrote to that effect to the Calcutta newspapers. The officers, too, were flattered, wept over and cajoled by the men to such an extent that any native would at once have suspected them. Not so, however, the poor confiding Englishman. To the last they trusted to the soldiers' honour, a sentiment which they forgot does not exist in the Asiatic breast.

* This party of only about 200 men was led by Major Vincent Eyre.

One evening, after the excitement of the day was over and everything apparently quiet, the officers met in the mess room. The party was unusually large for a native regiment, being augmented by a number of unposted ensigns.

The dinner was served as usual, and though there is little doubt that the mess servants knew what was coming not one scoundrel gave a hint.

Dinner half over, the alarm sounded, and as every one started from his seat and rushed to the doors, they were met by volley after volley, fired by their own men.

Fifteen of these victims of treachery were shot down, and the survivors scattered and fled.

Hampton was wounded slightly in the leg and more severely in the arm, but with a few others, among whom was his chum, rushed back into the mess room and escaped by a side entrance. Darkness favoured them and they made for the river, into which, maddened by despair, they dashed, and after fearful exertions managed to reach the shore near the fort, to the gates of which they had hardly strength to crawl.

Thus far they were safe, but they had many trials to encounter before the end of that troublous time.

The dastardly mob of sepoys joined the rabble of the town in murdering every European they met or could ferret out, and by next day the work of slaughter was finished. The little garrison of the fort had not only to contend against semi-starvation and disease in its most appalling forms, but they had to watch the native troops quartered with them, consisting

18

of four hundred Sikhs and a company of the very regiment which had mutinied. These last had possession of one of the gates, and the wonder is that they did not at once betray their post. They were, however, disarmed, and turned out, the Sikhs were persuaded to encamp outside under the pretence of making more room for the fugitive women within the ramparts, and after they left the defenders breathed more freely.

The weather was fearfully hot, and deaths by sunstroke were frequent. Cholera too, broke out and half the fighting men were carried off by it, as well as numbers of women and children.

After undergoing the most trying privations, the fort was relieved by Major Neil at the head of a handful of the Madras Fusiliers, with whom he had pushed on from Benares. After some days further reinforcements arrived and the garrison was able to march out and take vengeance on the cowardly foe who had gathered round them by thousands.

Youth and a good constitution aided Hampton in his recovery from his wounds. In a month or so he, with the remnant of the officers whose regiment had mutinied, were enabled to join Neil and Havelock's column, and share in all the glories of the campaign which ended in the relief of Lucknow.

CHAPTER XIV.

THE SIEGE—THE TIMELY DELIVERANCE—FINALE.

WHEN the chances of Neelapore being attacked became daily greater, the residents took shelter in the strongest built house in the station, and fortified it to the best of their ability. All the trees for a hundred yards round were cut down, provisions were laid in, and, in humble submission to the will of the Almighty, the little band awaited the result.

The planters of the district had been warned to combine for mutual protection : this they did at one or two of the most defensible points ; and about twenty joined the party at Neelapore.

It was a pitiable sight to see them come in, young and old, in crowded conveyances ; for when the rains are delayed till late in June, the heat is terrible beyond conception, and travelling by day is never in ordinary times attempted.

Some of the men were mad enough to drive with the hoods of their buggies down, or in open dogcarts ; and on their arrival at their destination, found their faces raw and blistered, as if by actual contact with fire; but the excitement was so great, the wish to place their families in security so absorbing, that the deadly effect of the sun was nearly forgotten.

One buggy load was such a mixture of tragedy and comedy that we are tempted to describe it.

Fancy, then, a white horse, which had been bathed in sweat, and then gradually covered over with a coating of dust. On slackening its paces, this had dried into large dirty patches. Down its face rolled two muddy tears, its head hung to the ground, and its flanks heaved distressingly. Out of the vehicle it had been dragging jumped a short, stout man, dressed in a loose flannel suit, with a pith hat, the brim of which was so broad, the crown so high, and the shape so suggestive of Bedlam, that the wildest imaginings of our English readers will fail to picture it.* *Indians*, however, will recognise an old friend at once. The wearer had fiery red hair and whiskers, with a face to match, and was evidently of an irascible temperament. Next descended a tall, gaunt, dark woman, his wife, whose bonnet and hair were in such a state that a little more dishevelment, and a little more dust, would have fitted her exactly for the character of Madge Wildfire. She had been weeping bitterly, and suffering in-

* The sola or pith hat is worn in a variety of eccentric shapes, but it is a real blessing, as it combines the most extraordinary lightness, with strength, of any material in the vegetable kingdom.

tolerable agonies of mind on account of the little infant which is handed to her by its black wet-nurse, who has been coiled away at the foot of father and mother for those weary forty miles.

Let us lift the handkerchief from baby's face. Poor little thing! Only six weeks old, and it has travelled all through that terrible sun, a ray of which has hitherto never been allowed to shine upon it; and yet it opens its bright little blue eyes, and is as jolly as possible.

The advent of so many people certainly increased the power of defence, but it diminished the comforts of all; for the rooms of the house of refuge, though large, were not numerous: the ladies, therefore, gave up the idea of separate beds, and slept in parties of four or five on the floor, while the men had tents which were pitched close to the house.

Conrad Daymer, among others, was indefatigable in his endeavours to make it siege proof, and at last even the ladies took an interest in *our* fortifications.

Notwithstanding the warlike preparations which were being made, and which shewed that the inhabitants of Neelapore were in dread of being attacked unawares, the business of the station went on as usual, the gentlemen messing and sleeping at the rendezvous, their houses being shut up, and left in charge of a servant or two.

The fortified house stood on the banks of the beautiful winding lake of which we have spoken, and its garden-terrace, overlooking the water, afforded the inmates' an agreeable spot in which they might enjoy the comparatively cool evening air; for still no rain had fallen, and it was hot, *awfully* hot. The pleasure-boats lay idly at the steps, for there was not enough breeze in the evening to fill their sails, though it blew a gale of hot wind during the day; besides, who could tell, if they ventured out, whether a rifle ball from the wooded banks might not be stealthily aimed at them?

Sometimes a call would be made on Laura for her guitar and a song to cheer the lonely hours; but the music seemed to fall harshly on the ear, and the performer generally ended by abstractedly striking some low, melancholy chords, more in unison with the thoughts of those around her, than merry strains could possibly be.

"Laura, dearest Laura," said Conrad, one evening as they sat together after daylight had departed, and the faint light of the stars revealed objects in a dim, ghostly light, "how brave, how good you are, to cheer all around you with your hopeful voice. Oh, that this terrible trial were over, for I see that anxiety is wasting you day by day, and the sight almost drives me mad. I would rather that we had sunk together, and been at rest in the Hooghly, than that you should become the victim of these fiendish natives."

"Dear Conrad, it is not manly of you to say so; and if God in His kindness should deliver us from these straits, we shall enjoy all the more the many blessings which, perhaps, we have never hitherto fully appreciated."

A sad time, truly, for the youthful pair, for whom everything had worn such radiant hues but a short space before.

As yet, however, their trials were not to be compared with those experienced by the numerous victims to the relentless cruelty of the natives at many of the stations in the north-west provinces. They had still some faithful servants, who seemed to show no sympathy with the sepoys in their murderous animosity to their English masters, and even to the last moment it was hoped that the rebellion would not spread so far to the south. These hopes, however, proved fallacious, and in a short time, they were doomed to experience some of those horrors which can never be forgotten by the unfortunates who experienced them, but which have almost faded away, as does the hideous nightmare, from the memory of our countrymen.

Had there been no native troops at Neelapore, it is highly probable that no rising would have taken place, but unfortunately such was not the case, and there is no doubt that the capture and death by hanging of an emissary of the King of Delhi at Nadanpore, brought matters to a crisis. We have been told since by natives that the Mahomedan troopers of the irregular corps at the nearest military station to Neelapore, had sworn, that if the above man were hanged, they would, within two days, murder their officers and join the mutiny in a body, and it actually happened as

they had vowed. A troop of these irregular horseman stationed at Neelapore, was commanded by a gigantic Mahomedan, named Sureef Khan. He was six feet four in height,
and proportionately broad and strong, with a very sinister
look, quite at variance with his manner, which was intensely polite and obsequious. He had sworn upon the
beard of the collector of the station, who had, by-the-bye,
particularly fraternised with him, that, so far as he could
prevent it, no harm should come to any one; and the irregular cavalry throughout India having up to this time
been faithful, he was almost believed.

This half belief was, however, soon resolved into a
certain assurance of his treachery, in the following
manner:—One morning, Jayram, an old Hindoo servant
of Mr. Templemore's, begged him to come into the verandah, as he had something of importance to communi-
cate. "Sahib," he said, "last night out of curiosity, I crept
up to the sowars' (cavalry) encampment, and heard Sureef
Khan and one or two others discussing some news which a
secret messenger had brought them from the head-quarters
of their regiment. Oh, sir, I am almost afraid to tell you;
but they said the Major Sahib and his wife were shot while
driving round the parade ground, and that the rebellious
Mahomed Hassain, of Goruckpore, had offered a thousand
rupees for the Major's head. He was, therefore, decapi-
tated, and thrown by the road side, near the dead body of
his poor wife. They then killed the doctor and his family,

and burnt the house over them. After a little discussion, Sureef Khan proposed they should join the jail guards here, murder all the Europeans, and then divide the seven lacs (£70,000) in the treasury."

Mr. Templemore felt the sickness of death creep over him as he listened to the man's tale; but to betray any symptoms of fear would have been so impolitic that he thanked and rewarded him, and pretended not to quite credit his story. Alas! he had scarcely reached the breakfast room when a travel-stained messenger, who had been heavily bribed, came in with a note concealed in his hair. It was from Nadanpore, and said, "poor Major Holmes and his wife* were barbarously murdered two days ago, as were also Dr. Garner, his wife, and infant; one child, a girl, who was out walking with the ayah, was concealed in the house of a woman of bad character, and was saved." In fact, the note confirmed the old servant's account, and it concluded by stating that as soon as they could be spared a hundred Europeans would be sent to their aid.

As the news was whispered from one to another, the sad, fixed, look of despair stole over the faces of the unfortunates at Neelapore, the men solemnly swearing to fight to the last breath, and to shoot the women rather than allow them to fall into the hands of the natives.

* This lady was the daughter of Lady Sale, who was a prisoner among the Affghans, gave birth to a daughter there, lost her first husband, was remarried, and ended her eventful life as we relate; she used to behave like a mother to the men of her husband's regiment.

As we have mentioned before, the officials still attended
their different offices, and though everyone about the courts
knew what was brewing, they still went through the
mockery of respect and obedience to the officials. This
almost absurd state of things was at last brought to a close
by an attempt being made on the Judge's life, as he was
driving home from his court.

As usual with the natives, the assassination was well
planned but badly executed. A shot was fired from behind a tree, two or three men rushed up to the buggy,
and tried to cut down Mr. Templemore with their
tulwars: but he was driving too fast for them to make
sure of their aim, and the hood of the buggy warded
off their blows, while a few bounds of the high-spirited
blood mare took him past the danger, and he was so far
safe.

None of the natives about the courts, nor any of the
townspeople, came to sympathise with him or express their
regret at the dastardly attack; and it was seen by all that
matters had reached their crisis. That night the guard on
duty at the house of refuge were startled by the sudden
illumination of the sky in the direction of the Collector's
and Magistrate's houses, and men, women, and children
turned out to look at the awful sight, while the yells from
the mob, who were fairly let loose, echoed through the still
night air.

"There go all your things, Harrington," said some one

to the Magistrate; "and now there's another fire—that must be Edwards's house."

The two poor men and their wives looked on in a kind of stupor, at the destruction of every valuable they had, and strange to say, seemed almost indifferent, so absorbed were they in the thoughts of what might happen to-morrow.

The first act of the insurgents was, of course, to let the jail-birds loose, and their next to take possession of the treasury. Here, however, a slight hitch in the arrangements took place, as the cavalry claimed more than their share. At last it was settled that the boxes of treasure should not be touched till all the Europeans had been killed, and then a fair division should be made. All the property in the different houses in the station was looted, and the collector's great friend, the arch-scoundrel, Sureef Khan, open that gentleman's wardrobes, and took everything of the best for himself, down to—and this annoyed him most —his Shetland wool stockings.

Early in the morning, after burning and destroying everything belonging to their masters, a disorderly onslaught was made on the house. Headed by a few of the bravest, they attempted to carry it by a sudden rush, but the besieged being all sportsmen, were first-rate shots, and knocked over the leaders like nine-pins, before they reached within fifty yards. The result was that the besiegers retreated, vowing terrible retribution for their losses.

They now seemed to change their tactics, and no more

assaults were made, but their new method of attack was much more harassing. They took possession of all the outhouses which covered the approaches to the wells, and dug trenches on either side of the compound which led down to the lake, from which they could fire on any one going down for water, thus preventing the besieged from procuring any. The supply of provisions was entirely cut off, and the store they had laid in was now all they had to depend upon. Only three or four native servants remained, and the poor ladies helped in the cooking and all the menial duties.

Volleys were fired every now and then at the doors and windows, but as these were all half bricked up, and the upper portions protected by mattresses and rubbish of every description, no harm was done.

The heat inside now became awful, and it was lucky that at night the wretched defenders could creep up the turret stairs to the terraced roof, to enjoy the cool night air. This, although refreshing, brought on fever with some, and the likelihood of a pestilence breaking out in a place so crowded became more and more imminent. No letters were of course received, and our friends could not tell what steps were being taken to relieve them.

As day after day passed without a sign, they began to fear that the messenger they had despatched to Nadanpore on the night of the conflagration had betrayed them, and to add to the horrors of their position, they became aware that the natives were mining their way to the house. They had a long distance to dig, but it was quiet slow work, just suited to their character, and was likely to be successful without involving much risk. The besieged now attempted to countermine, but they were perfectly unskilled in such matters, and could not for a time ascertain the real direction of the gallery.

In the mean time the duty of watching this, and being contantly ready for a rush, so fatigued them that they could hardly stand, and it was seen that unless assistance came speedily, exhaustion, bad food, and vitiated air would forestall the enemy. The water, too, was fast disappearing, and they were now living on rice and dall (dried peas), the live stock, consisting of fowls, having been soon consumed. The poor women became utterly regardless of appearances, and the men, blackened with gunpowder and pale as ghosts with the heat, were hardly to be recognised.

The house had been so well protected and was so massively built, that up to this time none of its defenders had been wounded, but the privations and suffocating atmosphere had already prostrated many of the women and children. The latter suffered the most, and the poor little baby which we have mentioned died in Laura's arms, its mother lying unconscious from fever. It was buried just outside the walls during the night, mid solemn silence, and the burying party escaped without being fired on.

Conrad Daymer was frenzied when he looked on Laura,

and saw her loved face day by day becoming more death-like, and he determined to make one effort to save her and the garrison. He proposed to Mr. Templemore and the others that he should slip out disguised, and make the best of his way to Nadanpore for assistance. The old servant, Jayram, whom we have already mentioned, upon being interrogated as to the route, said that his house lay about half way between the two stations, and that he was willing to accompany Conrad. His offer was thankfully accepted, and with the aid of a suit of his clothes, and a plentiful smearing of lamp black, turmeric, and oil, Conrad was converted into a very disreputable-looking native.

At midnight the lovers bade each other what perhaps might be their last adieu, but necessity is a stern master, and strengthened by despair, the one begun his task with a hopeful heart, while the other resigned herself in tearful agony to the will of Providence.

It was arranged that the besieged should attract attention to the front of the house, and while the usual fusilade consequent on any movement was going on, Conrad and old Jayram should creep down to the edge of the lake, and getting into the old canoe moored there, should lie down in it, and paddle with their hands only, and thus silently pass down beyond the line of sentries, whose attention would doubtless be attracted to the commotion in front.

Laura and one or two others, crouching on the terrace, with scarcely beating hearts and bated breath, saw the two dark forms glide down to the water, and did not cease to watch for any movement on that side which might betoken the miscarriage of the scheme, till the signal that all was well struck plainly on their eager ears. It was the prolonged scream of the jackal (uttered by Jayram) which the natives can imitate to the life. One prayer for their success, and our heroine and her companions stole down again to comfort the sick and tend the dying.

It was wonderful to see the patience and resignation of the women under all the trials they had to undergo, and there is no doubt that the heroic attitude sustained by all, through the withering storms of that calamitous year, wonderfully raised the prestige of England's sons and daughters in the eyes of the merciless natives.

After Conrad's departure, the garrison calculated the amount of food left in store, and it was found that they must curtail their already insufficient meals to enable them to hold out for another week.

The expression of feelings of misery has a limit, and when the worst was known, no remarks were made; a deep-drawn sigh from one, or a long look at those he loved from another, were all the outward marks of despair. Day by day those of the ladies who had been able to work for the rest were deprived of one or two of their members, and those who still could crawl about had double duty to perform. Poor Laura's youth and short residence in India still carried her through every trial, but her aunt, and many others, were struck down from the very first from fright, and she now lay in an alarming state of exhaustion and low fever.

The operations of the miners, although frustrated once or twice, still continued, and lacking any scientific knowledge of such things, the besieged wasted a great deal of time and strength in their ill-directed efforts to avert the danger. Besides this, the foundations of the house were deep and strong, and presented formidable obstacles to the wearied hands who had to break through them to commence the countermines. Their only hope lay in succour arriving in time. They hardly considered that Nadaupore itself was in a very precarious state, placed on one side of a large Mahomedan town, which would undoubtedly have risen had our arms been unsuccessful in the North West. But how could they judge fairly; they only knew they were in desperate straits, and hope's sweet angel, the last always to quit poor sorrowing mortals, still hovered over them and cheered them with her smile.

Two days more passed away—still no help. The strongest now gave in, and very few shots were fired in answer to the volleys which the fresh relays of besiegers poured into the battered doors and windows. The women were all huddled away on the side of the house remotest from the supposed direction of the last mine. Those of the men who could hold their guns sat watching the place, but with little hope of being able to withstand their assailants if it did succeed.

At last a loud but muffled report told that it was sprung, and was followed by a tremendous yell from the infuriated fiends around them. A large verandah and two rooms came down with a crash, and the air was darkened by a cloud of dust. The besiegers made a rush, but were met by a volley from the few desperate defenders of the breach, who, now that they were exposed, lost two of their number, and had to retire into the shelter of the nearest room. There was a hesitation for a moment or two in the attack. A short silence, when, merciful Heavens!—can it be? It is, it is! —an English cheer.

The cowardly rabble are taken unawares; they fly like sheep, and are bayoneted in scores. A few of the deliverers are mounted, and cut up the fugitives, who scatter in every direction.

In half an hour the fight is over.

Who shall describe the feelings of gratitude of that poor hunger-stricken band, or the joy of their deliverers to think that they had been in time. In time, but not for all. Two of the ladies lay dead in one corner, and one or two more were not expected to survive.

"Let us try to save those who still live," said the medical man who accompanied the party, and fifty willing hands tore open the windows and doors, and allowed air to enter the house.

Conrad, who had been in the thickest of the fight, and was covered with blood and blackened with powder, rushed

19

madly to find Laura and was horror stricken when he saw the ravages that the last few days had made in her and her companions.

She folded him proudly in her arms and thanked God that he was safe, while he, still hot from the strife, could not repress his almost savage exultation at the retribution which he had aided in bringing down on the authors of such a pitiful scene.

The joy of their meeting was however clouded by anxiety about Mrs. Templemore, who seemed in the last stage of weakness, hardly recognising Conrad when he knelt at her bed-side, and in whispered accents told her to be of good cheer.

A day or two more of hardship and she must have succumbed, but after a week's nursing she began to rally, and then her recovery was rapid.

Conrad insisted on Laura placing herself on the sick list with her aunt, and constituted himself head nurse and comforter to both of them, and great was his joy and satisfaction when, after a week's care, he could take out his patients for a gentle drive.

Mr. Templemore was terribly altered, and looked ten years older, but he had stood the trial better than most of his companions, and sooner recovered from its effects.

In following the fortunes of Conrad, we had almost forgotten old Jayram who was thanked and fêted all over the station and became such an authority in all matters, that the native officials of the different courts sent him heavy presents as propitiatory offerings, with humble requests that he would use his influence to have them reinstated in the judge's favour. The old fellow took everything that came, quite coolly, gave his moustache an extra curl, put on a resplendent gold necklace, laid in a small barrow load of brass cooking utensils, and a stock of new clothes, of which the most modest colours were canary and scarlet, bought a long-tailed ambling pony, and sent home orders to his native village by a trustworthy relation to feed all the Brahmins for four miles round, and to look out for a nice little girl of twelve or fourteen years of age, whom he would honour with his hand, when next the marrying months came round. The old man had acted splendidly throughout, and Conrad, in recounting the story, candidly confessed that without his aid, he never could have accomplished his task. He was first taken by his guide to his village, where he procured him a hearty meal of milk and rice, and persuaded him to rest for three hours. He then either stole or borrowed a couple of ponies, and with blankets for saddles, they rode into Nadanpore. Here they heard of Niel and Havelock's victories, and were able to secure two hundred Europeans and twenty mounted volunteers. With these they pushed on night and day, but they had to keep together, and it was the third morning before they could reach Neelapore.

It hardly needed the defeat they had experienced to make

the besieging parties disperse in all directions, for they also had heard of the success of the British arms in the North West, and had intended to make for Oude so soon as they had massacred the garrison of Neelapore.

In the course of a week or two the force at Mr. Templemore's disposal enabled him to punish those of the townspeople of Neelapore who had joined in the rising, as well as those of the native officials who had not fled the country. Some of those who remained, and at the best had been but neutral, now came forward and proved in the most satisfactory manner, that even had the European troops not arrived, they had made arrangements to raise the siege. Of course they were not believed. The scales had fallen from the eyes of every civilian in India, and although it was impossible to punish all concerned, the authorities had their own ideas on the subject, and the natives could tell by the look and gesture of their rulers, that the time for trifling had gone by.

The actual inhabitants of the district had certainly not joined in the attack on the station; but if they had chosen they might easily have raised a force which would have scattered the jail-guards and the irregular cavalry, who were the leaders in the outbreak.

When the large landed proprietors saw that the British star was again in the ascendant, they were profuse in their expressions of loyalty and regret at the indignities suffered by the officials of their district; and the Government had to accept their apologies for non-action with the best grace it could.

After Mrs. Templemore and Laura had recovered a little, Conrad gave them an account of all he had heard at Nadanpore, especially with regard to Desmond. "Poor misguided fellow," he said, "he is no more. He shunned every one after the exposure about his wife, and when his regiment met the enemy, he evidently only wished to throw away his life. At one of their attacks on a fortified village, the stronghold of the defenders was a Mahomedan mosque, which a few desperate men held to the last. Not having guns with them, the only method of dislodging the occupants was by blowing open the door. This Desmond volunteered to do with his own hand, and after he had succeeded, rushed in upon the enemy, when he was cut to pieces, before his men could overpower the band of desperadoes."

"Did you hear anything about poor Mr. Struggles?" said Laura.

"Yes," replied Conrad. "He never had an opportunity of revenging himself on his sheristadar, as that worthy quietly poisoned himself when his house was surrounded by a party sent out to surprise him. He has resigned the service, and leaves shortly for England. He says that, what with "competition civilians, railways, and European interlopers of all kinds, India is no longer a fit place for a man of family to remain in."

By the end of the rains the rebellion was stopped in its

progress, and all the lower provinces of Bengal returned to their usual quiet state. Communication was restored with the up country stations, and Laura heard, every now and then, from Hampton, who had joined the small body of volunteer cavalry which accompanied Havelock's column to Cawnpore and Lucknow, and in which he had greatly distinguished himself. He had been lucky enough to escape sun-stroke and wounds, and when the weather became cool, wrote in high spirits of his share in the different fights. He seemed also to have secured the friendship of those in power, and had been promised an appointment in the Punjaub.

As the bracing north winds of the cold weather began to blow on the plains, Mrs. Templemore and Laura once more looked themselves again. They had indeed passed through the valley of the shadow of death, and many a day of peace and quiet must pass before their minds could recover the dreadful shock they had received; but in a calm, placid way, they were happy, and thankful when they considered how many homes had been made miserable, while all the members of *their* family had been spared.

And now, with reluctant hand, we must lay our last sketch before our readers. It is one over which we linger with more than ordinary interest, for in it we must bid adieu to all the friends whom we have accompanied through so many perils, and wish "God speed" to our gentle Laura.

It is a bright, breezy morning in the month of February. The mimic waves are dashing on the shore, or curling themselves into tiny breakers on the sparkling bosom of the Neelapore Lake. The trees are beginning to shew their bright green leaflets, and the fields glow with the dazzling contrasts presented by the different bright-coloured crops which flourish under the tropical sun. The roads are covered with crowds of gaily dressed natives (who are more obsequious and polite than ever), with heavily-laden carts, elephants, strings of camels, droves of little knock-kneed, humble-looking donkeys, files of milkmen trotting in with their wares slung on their shoulders by bamboo yokes, richly clothed grandees in palankins, fakeers with no clothing at all, goats, dogs, cows, old women, toddling children, and the fifty other component parts of the scene presented by the main road of a native town on a fine, cold weather morning. Through the tangled mass comes driving an English carriage and pair and several buggies, which are whirling along to the tune of twelve miles an hour.

But what means all this gathering of vehicles in the Judge's compound, this rushing to and fro of snowy-garmented servants, and this constant arrival of guests? Why are all the gates and verandahs festooned with flowers? and why in the dining-room this tremendous long table, laid out for at least fifty?

As we enter the lofty drawing-room, our questions are answered at a glance.

Here, in the centre of a group of friends, stands Laura in her bridal dress, with Conrad beside her. He looks supremely happy, and as he, ever and anon, bends down to whisper softly to her, almost touches the orange blossoms in her wreath with his lips. Near them are Mrs. Blandon and her charming daughters, all looking as lively as if the atmosphere of marriages had some peculiarly exhilarating effect. They are come up from Calcutta to spend a month with Mrs. Templemore, and the young ladies are to officiate as bridesmaids. Gaily talking to them is Hampton Templemore (down on a fortnight's leave of absence), bronzed, moustached and bearded, with such a dashing, take-you-by-storm look that it is the sisters' turn now to guard the citadels of their hearts, and we really do believe this time he will settle which one it is to be.

Mr. Templemore looks as rosy and as little like an Indian as ever, and, forgetting all the troubles he has gone through, is laughing and joking merrily. His wife, pale, delicate, and exquisitely dressed, is radiant with smiles as she receives the felicitations of her friends.

Now the clergyman is ready. The youthful pair plight their troth, and, after receiving the congratulations of the party, Conrad proudly leads his blushing bride into the banqueting room. The champagne corks fly in all directions, toast follows toast, cheer echoes cheer. Here is the carriage at the door. One cheer more—a hundred good byes. Now for the old slippers—that's right. Crack goes the whip, the horses bound forward, and they are off, with whom do you think tucked up behind in the dickey?—why old Jayram, who saved the garrison, and who is to be provided for by Conrad for the rest of his days.

THE END.

PRINTED BY F. C. HARRISON, QUEEN'S TERRACE, ST. JOHN'S WOOD.